ALONE IN THE DARK

Fig. 1. Detail from Hieronymus Bosch, *Ship of Fools* (1490–1500)

First published in 2024 by punctum books, Earth, Milky Way.
https://punctumbooks.com

ISBN-13: 978-1-68571-160-3 (print)
ISBN-13: 978-1-68571-161-0 (ePDF)

DOI: 10.53288/0475.1.00

LCCN: 2024935765
Library of Congress Cataloging Data is available from the Library of Congress

Book design: Hatim Eujayl
Cover design: Vincent W.J. van Gerven Oei
Cover photograph: *Wheat Stubble South of Thurman, 1965.* © Robert Adams, courtesy of Fraenkel Gallery, San Francisco.

spontaneous acts of scholarly combustion

HIC SVNT MONSTRA

Doug

Dibbern

Alone in the Dark

*Cinephilia and
the Heroic Imagination*

p.

Contents

Acknowledgments

I'd like to thank Eileen Fradenburg Joy, Vincent W.J. van Gerven Oei, SAJ, Hatim Eujayl, and Livy O. Snyder at punctum books, Ben Stewart and Tania Friedel for giving me advice on my last book (for which I forgot to thank them last time), and Beth Boyle Machlan, Jenni Quilter, and Richard Scott Larson for giving me feedback on this book. Thanks, friends.

In the snake carriage, past
the white cypress,
through the flood
they drove you.

But in you, from
birth
foamed the other source,
on the black
shaft of memory
dayward you climbed

— Paul Celan

1

Aesthetic Compulsion ::
Euphoria and Degradation

My oldest memory is that the image is filled with mud. Mud in the black foreground, blotched with puddles that mirror the pale, eggshell-gray air, stretches through the flat expanse of the gray middle ground, one long pitted and scarred smear, to the dull gray of the background where a concrete building, exhausted by the decades it's lorded over this lifeless yard, seems inclined to meet its end, to return to the horizon once more the power to delimit the mud's faint congress with the sky. Every once in a while, the wind picks up in listless, spiraling drifts, its minimalist audio reiterations reminding us that there must be something beyond the edge of the frame, that this landscape must keep spreading, must keep replicating, so that we're surrounded, image upon image, the ameliorating vision of Europe's nineteenth century collapsed in upon itself into the numb discoloration of this visual field.

Then, finally, after these charged seconds have suffused the theater with a grim anticipation, one skinny cow peers out from the building and steps out into the mud. And as the camera remains frozen in place a hundred feet away, the animal's hesitant curiosity about the brown image she's just entered makes

15

clear that it will not be her exploration, but the swelling and unfolding of senseless time that will be the subject of this film. Then another cow, then another, then bulls with inch-long horns begin to appear — slowly, slowly — until a dozen or so of the ragged beasts congregate, unsure, lowing into the incessant wind, seconds piling upon seconds, minutes piling upon minutes.

The cows stand by idly, one bull tries and fails to mount his neighbor, a few wander in circles, until eventually, one by one they head screen left, and the camera, so leisurely and smoothly at first that we barely notice, glides along with them, making us unconsciously perceive this movement as a miracle, making this experience of a nothingness pregnant with itself onscreen the only reprieve that this world — this art form — can afford us, enabling us now to cast our gaze over this farm's glorious dilapidation — water barrels rusting against pocked and peeling concrete walls, ceaseless puddles and slurry grooves, telephone lines that crisscross the cloudless ashen sky, leafless trees like watermarks of thorns — till the cows, plodding along in the distance, disappear behind brick buildings and wooden fences as the camera continues to drift leftward, then emerge again, then disappear behind another wall's cracked surfaces for so long we begin to suspect that there is nothing and will be nothing anymore in this movie but the scarred face of this century-old brick until the cows reappear from behind the buildings once more and come to a standstill in a new field of mud, as vast and pointless as the first — emblems of impermanence at variance with the infinite stretch of the landscape and the sky — milling about listlessly once again before they move off to disappear behind the far corner, and the eight-minute-long tracking shot finally and mercifully comes to an end.

It was a cold afternoon in January, 1998. I was sitting alone in a darkened theater at Lincoln Center in New York, watching the Hungarian director Béla Tarr's seven-and-a-half-hour magnum opus *Sátántangó*, only the second time it had screened in New York, and the word from the few journalistic outposts in that pre-Internet age and from the chatter among my few cinephile friends was that this obscure film by this obscure Eastern European auteur might just be *the* mysterious masterpiece of the decade. The memory of this movie — or perhaps even more the memory of submerging myself into it, of having lived through it, of having been the type of person who knew of its existence and mustered the courage or the folly to have actually endured the experience — became a touchstone for me.

I was 27 and I'd been sinking into an obsession with the movies that had begun to change me, helping me formulate to myself the type of person that I wanted to become. I'd begun to suspect, in fact, that my burgeoning mania for the art of the cinema was more a means of shaping a new identity than it was exclusively a love of the medium. There was something about *Sátántangó*'s baroque vision of austerity that struck a chord with me. There was something about its challenge to the limits of cinematic style, its exploration of the extreme frontiers of the filmic representation and magnification of time's elasticity, its exhaustive examination of the boundless sprawl of the quotidian, something about its fervent interest in degradation and despair, that appealed to my emerging sensibility, reminding me of art's power to make us see not so much the world it represents but our own self through it, to mirror our desires and dreams, and to enable us to bask in the act of self-definition.

As the film toiled through its glacial unfurling, it did eventually take on the outlines of a story, following the residents of a tiny and impoverished communal farm, an insular village that is more Tarr's idea of the human condition than it is of Hungary's experiment with communism: a man is having an affair with a neighbor's wife; men are plotting to steal other villagers' money; an alcoholic doctor spies on his neighbors; the town decides to pack up and leave to build a new collective farm somewhere else. But decades later — even after sitting through the entire seven-and-a-half hour film on three more occasions — the plot and the characters are not what I remember or cherish. In fact, I don't care the least bit about them.

No. I remember only the granularity of the image, its multitude of funereal shadows, its pitch-black silhouettes of figures cast against an almost fibrous sky, the five-minute-long shot of a woman's back as she sits at a shabby table looking out through a smeared window, the five-minute-long shot of a man's back as he sits at a similarly shabby table looking out a similarly smeared window at the incessant rain and puddles reflecting the charcoal sky and the black, shit-like mud that rises up from the bottom of the image to push against the mere sliver of gray sky struggling to make itself visible at the top of the frame, minutes-long tracking shots of a pair of men, their backs to us, trudging through a deserted street past abandoned, dilapidated concrete buildings with howling wind behind them raising trash and crumpled newspapers to envelop them inside a cyclone of filth, the same men in a minutes-long tracking shot now walking toward us through a flat, empty landscape of grassless and treeless fields in a tempest of rain, landscapes of barren earth and scraggly leafless trees and gray vacant skies, landscapes bisected into swaths of dark gray sky and the slightly darker oily gray sludge of the earth, unremitting torrential rain, wet dogs and wet pigs drinking from rain-splattered puddles, minutes-long tracking shots of the village's doctor — with his hunched shoulders and pockmarked, flabby face disappearing inside his overcoat — stumbling drunk through an almost black copse of birches while even-blacker smoke wafts in the distance behind another line of birches on the horizon, unrelenting tracking shots through the woods, unrelenting tracking shots in emptied acres of dirt, unrelenting tracking shots through the muddy village, the intensity and depth of the blackness and the hollowed-out, echoing ambiance of the grays, the eight-year-old girl grim and already resolutely lost and hopeless and vehemently antagonistic toward the world around her wearing an oversized coat trudging alone through the village mud, the girl sitting alone in a dusty attic looking through a small window out over the gray and empty and grassless fields, lying on her back on the dusty floor of the attic pulling her cat close, holding the cat fiercely by the skin of the neck so that the cat is paralyzed with fear, then rolling over and over again with the cat outstretched in her arms so that the cat squeaks and yawls to get free but the girl keeps

Fig. 1. Screenshot from *Sátántangó* (dir. Béla Tarr, 1994).

rolling over and over, kicking up sawdust clouds, the cat mewl-
ing and screaming, but the girl, cruel and insistent, keeps rolling
over and over again for minutes on end, later walking toward
us through the woods holding her dead cat in her arms in what
must have been a three-minute or five-minute or nine-minute-
long backward tracking shot, later spying through a window on
six or seven villagers dancing drunk at night in dizzying spirals
to accordion music in a seedy bar in a scene that seems to go on
for ten minutes or twenty or thirty, a scene that wants to explode
the film itself both into and out of its own boundlessness, then
vacant, treeless landscapes, dirt roads leading over a ridge to
nowhere, an empty forest glade invaded by mist — a probing
and ritualistic mist, mist like a consciousness, a mad cartogra-
pher's vision of whole continents of mist, mist like the nimbus
of an absent god — then another extreme close-up of the girl's
haunted blank expression in another minutes-long backward
tracking shot, her face a ceramic shroud, unwilling or unable to
comprehend that she has just murdered her cat, the only thing
she could possibly have loved in this oceanic charnel ground
of a village which is the whole world, close-ups of haggard,
drunken, wrinkled, unshaven, alcoholic faces, the villagers liv-

ing in dingy isolation, their backs turned to us, cramped spaces with dirty mattresses, filthy plates and cups, creaking wooden furniture, smudged windows, lone light bulbs dangling from the ceiling, the villagers walking in a five-minute-long tracking shot, their backs to us, the wheels of their suitcases on the gravel road taking over the soundtrack like a ceaseless round of gunfire, and the incessant swirling wind like the sound of metal scraping against metal from miles away, and the incessant rain, and the puddles reflecting the gray sky, and the mud that rises like excremental furrows to the top of the frame so that we can see only a fragment of the gray and hopeless sky (fig. 1).

Eight-and-a-half hours and two intermissions after that eight-minute-long tracking shot of cows ambling through the mud of an abandoned farm that started the film, after the very last shots — of the village doctor in a minutes-long tracking shot walking alone through an empty, dark gray, flat, and treeless plain against an impenetrably gray sky, and later, of the doctor alone in his suffocating living room hammering nails to board up his rain-spattered window from the inside in order to isolate himself ultimately and irrevocably in his interior darkness, safe from the darkness of the outside world, thereby replicating the metaphorical relationship we spectators have been having with the outside world ourselves throughout the entire length of this seven-and-a-half hour film — in the darkened theater, well past midnight, the credits began to roll, and a tentative smattering, then a more confident applause rose, then spread like the movie itself, the way thunder can announce itself from behind distant hills, until the applause was an ovation, and the credits came to an end and the theater lights came on and we all realized that people across the auditorium were standing, had been standing, and that I too was standing, and we were clapping and cheering and hollering toward a bright, now empty screen for the benefit of no one but ourselves. And then, from behind a curtain at the back of the stage, a tiny figure emerged: bent over, unshaven, wizened, thin wisps of hair hovering like flickers of electricity over a balding scalp, the iconic image of the Eastern European intellectual, a face that appeared to have inhaled two million cigarettes, and everyone in the audience understood instantly that this must be him — that it could be no other — that it must be Béla Tarr himself, and the audience roared. People were stomping their feet. And Tarr lumbered forward, raised a hand to acknowledge us, nodding with grim recognition.

Then, out of the corner of my eye, just a few feet ahead of me from her customary position in the exact center of the third row — the true home of the cinephile, she'd said — a second figure made the flair of her existence known, clambering over the people sitting to her left to push her way to the aisle as if her skin were on fire, then leaped up the three steps onto the stage so that everyone could now see that it was, in fact, her — it could be no one other, after all, with her pulsating aura and that shock of white stripe through her coal black mane — Susan Sontag, who seemed in that moment to shoot herself out of a cannon across the stage to embrace Tarr in a bear hug, and the crowd and I erupted in a feral coruscation of applause, well past midnight in the coldest depths of January, celebrating not just Tarr who made *Sátántangó*, not just Sontag for her status as our iconic representative, the exemplar of our own intellectual ambition, but also ourselves, for having experienced *Sátántangó*, for having sunk into it, for having endured it, as if sitting alone, immobilized, in a darkened room for seven-and-a-half hours living through this experiment in cinematic excess, this audiovisual rendition of anguish, gazing into the muddy infinity of the land and into the cloudless infinity of the gray sky that is the symbol of the void at the very heart of existence was not just an experience of watching a very long movie, but was, in fact, a heroic intervention into the turning of the world.

§

The experience of watching *Sátántangó* — living on the fine line between ecstasy and oblivion — didn't exist in isolation, though. In those years when I was still young, in fact, I lived a diluted form of that experience almost every night. For years and years and years. When I was in my twenties and thirties, I went to the movies obsessively — six or seven nights a week, every week of the year, sometimes two or even three movies a day — taking the subway from one theater to another, which required elaborate planning and record-keeping consisting of revival house calendars, *Village Voice* and *New York Times* and *New Yorker* listings, and a dedicated pocket-sized movie-schedule notebook in which I'd meticulously list the starting time, title, director, country, year, and venue in blue ink, sometimes four or five possible options for a single day, always carrying my subway map with me, week after week, month after month, 350 feature films a year, year after year, 10,000–15,000 hours of my adult life sitting alone in the dark gazing up at images projected larger than life onto a screen.

And though I couldn't have articulated it to myself at the time, I can see now that my quest was not so much to see every movie ever made as it was the early stages of an attempt to define the type of person I was unconsciously yearning to become. I was sinking into the movies, but I was also sinking into an idea of the self. My exhilaration at Tarr's desolation and my quest to inhale the history of cinema were of one piece: I was slowly but determinedly laying claim to a persona distinct from the world I'd come from precisely because — like all of us — I needed to leave the past behind.

The week that I saw the Tarr film was as obsessive as every other, yet another week crammed with a catalogue of discoveries for a young cinephile at the beginning of his career, consisting mostly of the Classical Hollywood genre pictures and Western European art films that the revival houses made available to me back in the 1990s. I saw *Sátántangó* the day after I saw Rex Ingram's *The Four Horsemen of the Apocalypse* at the Museum of Modern Art, a slow-burning silent epic from 1921 that first made Rudolph Valentino a star, the same week I'd first seen Jean Renoir's *The Grand Illusion* from 1937 with its luxurious camera movements in cramped interiors, with Erich von Stroheim's sublimely grim and naughtily monocled visage and Jean Gabin's ruddy, working-class cheeks and tousled hair, Valentino in another early star vehicle, *Blood and Sand* from 1922, which was boring, Mary Pickford in the surprisingly dark 1918 melodrama *Stella Maris* where she plays both a young invalid whose parents have protected her from the evils of the world by forbidding her to leave their mansion and the young maid mired in poverty they've hired to care for her, both of whom fall in love with the same man, the 1937 version of *King Solomon's Mines,* a campy adventure yarn with Paul Robeson, from the period when he'd first begun his dalliance with the Communist Party, as the chief Ubompa fighting against the evil usurper of his throne, the one hour-long episode of Jean-Luc Godard's maddeningly incomprehensible but absolutely rhapsodic late essay film *Histoire(s) du Cinema* comprised of an argosy of images and clips from the history of the medium dissolving into and superimposed on top of each other so that the whole thing felt less like a movie and more like the experience of looking out from the inside of a shifting crystalline mass, accompanied by the relentless clamor of Godard's electric typewriter, punctuated now and then by some enigmatically monosyllabic grunts from the old man himself, while the following day I ventured out on the F train into yet another intensive film noir retrospective at Film Forum, where I caught a double feature almost every other evening, making discoveries and revisiting some old favorites, immersing myself night after night in the comforting conventions of amorality and nihilism, Robert Siodmak's *The Killers* from 1946 and Billy Wilder's *Double Indemnity* from 1944, the former's hard-bitten chiaroscuro interiors more alluring to me than the latter's more famous hardboiled dialogue by Raymond Chandler rewriting James M. Cain, then Frank Tuttle's *This Gun for Hire* from 1942 and George Marshall's *The Blue Dahlia* from 1946, both pleasant but forgettable, Siodmak's surprisingly good *Phantom Lady* from 1944 and *Criss Cross* from 1947, Lee J. Thompson's *Cape Fear* from 1962, Sam Fuller's *Shock Corridor* from 1963, followed by a side-trip back up to MOMA on the F train to see Fred Niblo's silent version of *Ben-Hur* from 1925, one of the greatest box office hits of the 1920s, the film that made Ramon Navarro a star, and then back down on the F train to Film Forum again to catch Orson Welles's apotheosis of the low-budget crime film, 1958's *Touch of Evil* for the sixth or seventh time — then as now my single favorite movie — with its three-minute-long opening crane shot that soared from the asphalt to the tops of buildings and down again, its moving camera that trespasses into and out of subterranean stripper bars and suburban apartments alike, its floating camera that crossed international boundaries, its extreme zoom-ins on bloated dead faces, eyes popping and tongues hanging out, its hyperbolic montage sequences and echoing, over-dubbed audio, a film whose baroque modernist aesthetics conjoined with tawdry pulp material epitomizes that unexpected admixture of complexity and crudity, of high art and low art that make movies the most intoxicating of all art forms, the perfect exemplar of what Richard Wagner had called the opera, the *gesamtkunstwerk,* the total artwork, the one artistic medium that most perfectly incorporated every other medium into itself. And after the film noir retrospective, it was back up on the 2 or 3 train to Lincoln Center, where I discovered the films of Miklos Jancso — then as now a woefully underrated virtuoso of the moving camera — in the same Hungarian retrospective that had introduced me to Tarr: first *The Round-Up* from 1966, about a Habsburg prison camp in the 1860s, then *The Red and the White* from 1967, about Hungarian soldiers fighting alongside the Bolsheviks in the Russian Civil War, a film where Jancso first experimented with a moving camera, a camera that didn't just track right or left, but which lifted off the ground on a crane, swooped over lines of troops with a Faulknerian sense of modernist authorial audacity, an electrifying week of discoveries of this old Hungarian auteur that culminated with *Red Psalm* from 1972, a cinematic epiphany, a film that felt like it had exploded from within the depths of an imagination I hadn't conceived could exist, a film about an 1890s peasant uprising in which Jancso dispenses with character, plot, and dialogue, and stages instead a symbolic re-enactment of events in which men and women dance and sing and move together in hypnotic phalanxes like an experimental cinematic ballet, in which Jancso's camera hovers, floats left then right then back again, penetrates into circles of dancing peasant men then swivels and pushes past them, like a consciousness levitating, examining, drifting in seemingly unending shots — three minutes, four minutes, five minutes — shots so long you lose track of when and where they began, shots so long that time itself takes on tactile qualities, as if time is expanding out into the theater auditorium like a field of melting amber — the masses as metaphor, history itself as a kind of thickness of the air, a viscous, subterranean liquid, time as a saline haze — peasants and soldiers and priests moving as if mesmerized in rows through choreographed sequences in open fields beside a series of low-lying brick farm buildings out on the Hungarian steppe, groups of peasants hunched together in a circle discussing the class struggle, dancing together, arms clasped around each other's shoulders, singing peasant songs, fiddlers and guitarists and violinists and accordionists stepping gently among them playing Hungarian and French and English folk tunes, lines of soldiers and the capitalist landowner circling them, while still farther out, men on horses thundering in the background in ever-widening circles or galloping suddenly in violent diagonals into the frame, the camera moving in and pulling out, meandering, exploring, a band of peasants migrating slowly across one empty field to the next, soldiers setting bonfires, peasant women in kerchiefs wandering out on their own until they become mere smudges near the horizon of a flat, wide, and open plain, smoke filling the screen, and horses, always horses in the background, galloping and swerving in and out of frame, the sounds of their hooves and panting behind the lines of soldiers that keep circling and surrounding the peasants as they keep dancing and music keeps playing and the camera keeps intruding and retreating so that the film feels like it can never end, in the same way that all movies never seemed to end and my moviegoing never seemed to end because in the weeks that followed, I saw Renoir's *La Bete Humaine* from 1938, Federico Fellini's *And the Ship Sails On* from 1983, Vittorio de Sica's *The Gold of Naples* from 1954, Gillo Pontecorvo's *The Battle for Algiers* from 1966, Hiroshi Teshigahara's documentary *Antonio Gaudí* from 1984, Stan Brakhage's experimental epic *Dog Star Man* from 1964, the

MGM musical *The Band Wagon* from 1953, which made my heart leap with joy, Sergei Eisenstein's *The Old and the New* from 1929 with its famously elaborate milk-separator sequence — so much more impressive than the Odessa Steps sequence from *Battleship Potemkin* — the 1924 silent pirate epic *The Sea Hawk,* the biggest box office draw of that year though now almost completely forgotten, starring the matinee idol Milton Sills, now completely forgotten, and on and on and on and on.

But sometimes I had to admit, standing on the subway platform waiting for a train on my way home back to Brooklyn, in those weary late-night hours, I had my doubts. Over the course of those long years that so often felt drifty and unreal — even those most electrifying moments, even in the eye of the hurricane of that collective euphoria at the end of *Sátántangó* — I had to admit to myself that maybe I was a bit concerned. I had to admit that maybe this was all a bit too much, that maybe I had gone off the rails somewhere, that maybe I was engaged in some sort of act of evasion.

Alone on the subway, as the ecstasy of Tarr's vision had subsided in the dark hours past midnight on the 1 train to the A train to the F train on my way back home to Brooklyn, going through the same motions as I did almost every single night back then after going to a movie, at a time in my life when I'd decided it made the most sense to totally submerge myself in an ever-expanding monomania, sitting in the almost-deserted train cars among the now silent drunken revelers, groggy late-night bodega workers, homeless men sleeping in the corner, elderly operagoers, each of us in a mindless drift, slumped in our seats or bent over not quite gazing at the floors strewn with empty plastic bottles and straws and plastic bags and crumpled pages from the *New York Post,* I had to admit to myself that my obsessive love of the movies may have come not from a conscious desire for exalted aesthetic experiences but may have been the product instead of unconscious forces beyond my control — primal drives that were, perhaps, a bit self-destructive.

Sometimes in the weak illumination of those late-night hours, the subway cars' bleak interiors struck me as an uncomfortable mirror image of the movie theater from where I'd just come — as if I'd lost myself in a maze, turning a corner to find myself back where I'd begun. I'd organized my entire life, it felt at times, into one ongoing cycle, moving from one dim enclosed space to another, sitting beside strangers, incommunicative, staring off into a distance. Sometimes, especially when I caught my reflection late at night in the subway glass, it seemed to me that the specific mode of our discontent forces us to seek solace, ironically, in the source of that very dissatisfaction, in the mirror image of our own oblivion.

Cinephilia was a means of constructing an alternative way of life, embracing an oppositional existence of technicolor rapture, of chiaroscuro delirium, but it was also a way of living through phantoms, feeling through illusions, experiencing epiphanies through disavowal, finding salvation through renunciation, avoiding — no, rejecting — the real world. And the path of the subway train, snaking its way beneath Manhattan, then under the East River on the way home, like the snaking trajectory of a minutes-long tracking shot through a symbolically bleak and empty landscape, had a spiritual dimension: it was a pilgrimage. The austere resignation of the journey felt oddly comforting to me; it brought me in touch with some of the values I'd absorbed from my childhood going to church. It was no surprise, in retrospect, that the movies that often spoke to me most ardently evinced a similar aesthetics of ascetic reserve I'd learned to subject myself to when I was growing up.

My obsession with the movies was as much about traveling to and from the theater as it was about the movies themselves. When I wasn't sitting alone in the dark at the movies, I was always in motion — almost, it seemed, as if I was running away from something as much as I was reaching toward some goal. I was on a quest that took me beneath and across the city — from an office job to a movie theater to home again and again — but barely seeing the city at all. I was barely aware of the environment, the real world, above or around me, living an ersatz existence transporting myself from one shabby interior to another. And I was ecstatic about the prospect of seeing images projected larger than life onto a screen, ecstatic about the images I was actually seeing, or ecstatic about the memory of those images as I rode alone in a train car snaking beneath the earth and the river on my way home. I was in the thrall of what seemed at the time the most sublime form of ecstasy, the ecstasy of seeing an alternative world, more dramatic and more concise and more meaningful than our own, the bliss of the fictive, of living within a simulacrum.

But yes, I had to admit that even then, I was concerned. And I was curious. The fact that I, or that anyone, would devote an entire day, one of their rare free weekend days, to sit alone in the dark staring up at images on a screen, and that I, or that any-one, would think that this was not just an enjoyable but a heroic endeavor, struck me sometimes as an unsettling refusal of life itself. The idea that I, or that anyone, would orchestrate their entire lives around this continual act of submission — not just to art itself, but especially to films that subjected their viewers to this depth of melancholy — that I, or that anyone, would try to derive pleasure by pleasure's very denial struck me sometimes as a troubling repudiation of the self, of one's own autonomy.

The entire situation was ironic. I was so clearly using movies, after all, to bolster my independence. But it was this rejection of the self in search of the self — perhaps the very essence of the religious impulse — that felt so natural to me. It was this very negation, I've begun to suspect decades later, that formed the roots of my aesthetic taste, that led me to embrace the art of excessive austerity and of nihilism.

§

Many of my friends at the time, when we huddled together in someone's kitchen or in a corner of a dive bar in what was then a just-gentrifying Brooklyn, would gently smirk when I talked about going to the movies so obsessively. Watching a film was a passive act, they'd suggest — the very antithesis of the creative impulse that defined the writer or the artist, which is what we all assumed we were trying to become. But no, I'd say. Looking at a work of art or listening to it, experiencing it, sinking into it and letting it seep back into you, changing you, I'd say, is just as much an act of creation as painting or writing or recording music. In those moments, I told them, when I stepped into the quiet, expectant theater before a screening of a film by an obscure auteur like Hiroshi Shimizu or Mohsen Makhmalbaf or Marcel L'Herbier, I felt like I was Roald Amundson bravely pushing his team of dogs through a ferocious sheet of slurry into the icy interior of the poles. And explorers, I'd remind them, are not just venturing out into new locations for their own benefit; they are, as well, simultaneously inscribing these places onto the map, reordering and reframing — just like a novelist or a painter — a larger community's capacities for seeing and thus for understanding the world. No, I'd insist: the work of the cinephile — and it was a form of labor — is just as creative as the work of the poet or the sculptor or the filmmaker.

But the experience of moviegoing — socially, technologically, and aesthetically — inspires a specific mode of creative response distinct from other media. The movie theater turns its adherents into isolated individuals, sitting immobile and silent in the dark. The movies themselves, meanwhile — with their colossal, disembodied faces assembled in relation to other colossal, disembodied faces by the poetic reconfiguration of space and time — induce in their spectators an oneiric reverie, as if they're floating above or beyond the phenomenal world. The medium inspires a ruminative state of consciousness, while the nature of exhibition guides that meditation toward the subjects of individualism and solitude, and a fascination with the utter darkness that yet might be pierced by a small, distant, and burning illumination.

This particularly moody style of introspection colors the moviegoer's aesthetic temperament and thus their character as well. We say that children are developing their own personalities, for instance, when they begin to cultivate idiosyncratic tastes. I like *this, this,* and *this,* they say, but not *that, that,* or *that,* and by doing so, they — and we — begin to validate their existence by distinguishing themselves from others through the force of desire. Aesthetic taste is one of the primary engines of individuality. So cinephilia does arise from a genuine love of the movies, but it's also a process for constructing a persona in opposition to the identity that the world has bestowed upon us without our permission — even if we're not consciously aware of the fact that we're doing so. We shape our new identities by organizing narratives for ourselves based on our aesthetic experiences just as filmmakers do by arranging scraps of images and sounds together to create a coherent story. Everyday experience turns us into memoirists, audiovisual essayists of the self.

We necessarily invent an idealized conception of ourselves, a heroic figuration; but we define this ideal in contrast with its antithesis that gave it birth. That is, because each medium shapes its aesthetic novitiates in specific ways, cinephiles of my generation invented their heroic image in opposition to a sense of scarcity that circumscribed their experience. On the surface, the cinephile life seemed to be all about acquisition: every week, I might add seven or eight more films to my catalogue of experiences. And yet, so much of the cinephile existence has surprisingly little to do with the movies at all: so much of my obsession was not about seeing movies, but about waiting sometimes for years or even decades to finally get the chance to see that rare gem that I'd been pining over — if, in fact, I'd ever get a chance to see it at all. One imagined one's identity, then, in the seemingly incompatible modes of attainment and conquest on the one hand, and resignation and disillusionment on the other.

Back in the day before international file-sharing collectives on the Internet, it was much more difficult to track down and see the movies that had begun to intrigue you. Movie buff friends would talk in hushed reverence about films that were almost impossible to see, movies that rarely screened at the revival houses, and were still inexplicably unavailable on video — movies like Vincente Minnelli's *Some Came Running* from 1958, for instance, with its carnival finale where psychedelic flashes of colored lights rather than a physical antagonist seemed to be hunting Frank Sinatra down to his death atop a heap of garbage, or Douglas Sirk's *Tarnished Angels* from 1957, with its Rembrandt-esque shadows, its discomfortingly angular, widescreen compositions, and Robert Stack's pent-up, volcanic rage. And there were entire realms of film history from across the globe we knew would probably never screen in the city: Mexican classical cinema, with hothouse melodramas by directors like Emilio Fernandez, early wuxia films from the Shaw Brothers in Hong Kong, Indian Parallel Cinema, and the erotic Pink Film movement in Japan that enabled radical auteurs like Nagisa Oshima, Yasuzo Masumura, and Koji Wakamatsu to bring forth their haunted vision. And then there were the holy grails of cinema: the lost original cut of Welles's *The Magnificent Ambersons,* or Jacques Rivette's *Out 1,* the thirteen-hour modernist film by the most obscure member of the French New Wave that had — according to legend — screened just once for an audience of forty people in 1971 and only two more times at a pair of European film festivals two decades later. As curious as any of us were, we knew that seeing the vast majority of movies from across the globe would always remain merely a dream. The history of film was a herculean sea, a vast, churning ocean of an absence — an absence, though, that fostered yearning and the imagination as well.

Anticipation, expectation, and patience were fundamental aspects of the moviegoing life. But even this self-denial — the negative concomitant to cinephilia's voracious acquisitiveness — felt heroic to me. Self-denial, after all, was a cornerstone of almost every spiritual enterprise and each of the major religions. And I had been raised in church; I had descended from a centuries-long line of Scandinavian Lutherans, a tribe well-known for their emotional and spiritual restraint. Lutheran church architecture stridently avoided any hint of ostentation: the more plain the edifice, the less distraction the parishioners would have communing with the magnificence of a God that they approvingly understood would never answer. The people I came from spoke quietly and infrequently. They did not strive for worldly accolades. They had no interest in material possessions. They kept their feelings in check, as any sensible person would. So the image of the Christian ascetic naturally made sense to me. Abnegation, it was well understood, was not a form of abuse, but of amelioration: stripping away one's unnecessary attachments purified the self, nurturing more acute states of awareness and knowledge, and surrendering one's autonomy, it had always seemed obvious to me, brought one closer to the divine.

Perhaps I was searching for new avenues of reverence in those days because everyday life in the material world was so dispiriting. Daily life in my twenties and thirties consisted mostly of psychic tedium. Like most people I knew, I had no career goals because every career seemed like a capitulation. Like most people I knew, I spent most of my waking hours sitting at a desk in front of a computer screen in a corporate office. Most of my day — as with most people I knew back in that burgeoning information age — did not consist of work, exactly, but of staring off vacantly into space avoiding the work that was right in front of me or pretending to do the work that was only occasionally there. Like most people I knew, I sat at a desk in an office or cubicle in front of a computer screen from nine to five or ten to six only so that I could make money to pay for food and rent so that I could sit in a corporate office from nine to five or ten to six so that I could make money to pay for food and rent, day after day, week after week, month after month, year after year, rolling out before me as far as I could see.

I spent years doing data entry in a building filled with sweatshops in a hollowed-out Brooklyn neighborhood of empty storefronts and abandoned warehouses. I'd sit immobile and stare into a computer screen hour after hour, day after day, nine to five or ten to six, five days a week, typing information from the backs of video cassette boxes and CD sleeves and press releases into a database. Then I got fired. Then I spent years in Midtown as a technical writer for a company that designed billing systems for the telecommunications industry, where I spent months and months writing a 600-page manual for a telephone company's database system, Orwellianly titled The Logos Project, then spent months and months with nothing to do, staring off in a stultifying daze, nervous and twitchy, spending hours and hours and hours every day pretending to be busy, constantly refreshing my screen, pacing around the office acting like I was searching for a missing fax, idling by the Xerox machine as I made photocopies of random pieces of paper I'd grabbed from the recycling bin, hiding in the bathroom, where I crouched in a stall hoping no one could find me, sitting at my desk gazing through a glass partition at quadrants of cubicles. Then I quit. Then I spent years as a software tester for a company that designed computer programs that taught children to read. I sat in a chair hour after hour after hour, staring into a computer monitor as I worked through the same screens over and over again, watching educational videos and reading texts and answering multiple choice questions, trying to track down software bugs, typing in multiple possible answers, playing out various scenarios of moving through the game, trying to catch it in a loop, taking elaborate notes and drawing elaborate charts and diagrams, calculating scores, bored out of my mind, despising every boss I ever had, dying to escape capitalism's psychic confines from the moment I sat down at nine or ten to the moment I got out at five or six. And then I'd leave the office and get on the subway and head to a movie theater. And there, sitting alone in the dark, staring at images larger than life up on screen, I'd sometimes get in contact once again with the burning need that had brought me there.

It was in the movie theater, after all, where I could feel the hint of love. It was in the movie theater where I felt mended and annealed. It was in the movie theater, for instance, where I first became obsessed with the actress Ida Lupino. And from the moment I first encountered her — in the 1951 film *On Dangerous Ground* directed by Nicholas Ray, up at Lincoln Center in the same theater I'd seen *Sátántangó* just one year before — it felt as if her spirit had imbued my own. Every movie hovers in a gray zone in which the people on screen with whom we become emotionally invested are always simultaneously the fictional characters and the actors who are playing them. But in certain particularly poetic films and with some especially penetrating performances, that line blurs and the aura of the stars comes to the fore. *On Dangerous Ground* was one such film. My emotional experience with that movie — and with Lupino and her fellow performers — has resonated so deeply with me that even though I've now seen it a handful of times, I can never remember her character's name or of any of the other characters in the movie. It's a sign of Ray's skills as a director and Lupino's force as an actor that to this day I cannot conceive of any of these characters by their fictional names but only as the stars themselves.

The moment that touched me most powerfully came in the charged climax of the film, when we see Lupino in a tight close-up, turning her eyes to the heavens, and offering a prayer up to God. In that scene, she draws on the entire aesthetic register of the medium to bring forth states of consciousness I wouldn't have recognized — or would have refused — on my own, eliciting sensations other than the desire for desolation that had resonated with me so vibrantly when I first encountered the work of Béla Tarr. She became, in that moment, my counterpoint to pessimistic despair. She became for me a messenger of undiluted compassion, a symbolic alternative to the nihilistic tendencies to which I often gave in, a complementary notion of the person I might possibly become.

I was moved by that close-up in that climactic scene partly because Ray had heightened Lupino's allure when he first introduce her earlier in the film by intentionally concealing her face. In her first scene, we initially look out from her position — indeed, it's as if we are her — at two vengeful, brutal men, played by Robert Ryan and Ward Bond, who've knocked at her front door. Instead of seeing her in a close-up, as most directors would have done, Ray allows us to understand her only by hearing her voice.

And her voice hangs in the air, as ethereal as vapor, a sign of her fragility, but with a husky alto timbre that hints at the depth of her character, her loneliness but also her pride, as if her voice emanates from some other empathic dimension inconsistent with the crude, snowbound landscape that surrounds her. Lupino deploys her body, as well, to emphasize both her brittleness and her resolve as she leads them into the interior of her living room, her psychic space, which is uncannily dim, lit only by a flickering fire. Ray intensifies her mystery by photographing her only from behind, keeping her face hidden from the two men and from us. Yet just by moving through her domestic interior — step by precise step — reaching to brush a hanging ivy, gently touching the mantel and a kettle above the fireplace, she manages to turn that darkened room, isolated in a snow-swept valley, into an arena dense with anticipatory dread. She manages, as well, through her inflexible torso and the hesitant precision of her steps, to imbue that space with a quivering vulnerability that we in the audience begin to feel along with her, the quiet ache which is the root of the human condition. So in that moment when she finally turns and we see her face for the first time, the film has already created the conditions of revelation: in that moment, we recognize ourselves in her because it is in that moment that we are finally able to see that she is blind.

This dichotomy between vision and speech, powerlessness and magnetic authority, echoes with other dichotomies that Ray sets up throughout the film, between vengeance and compassion, brutality and love, hopelessness and redemption. The film's other protagonist — Lupino's foil — is Robert Ryan. One of the two men whom she's invited into her living room, he had been up until that midway point, the film's central character: a violent, vicious cop from the city, six-foot-five, square-jawed, and embittered, with a bass baritone growl that carried with it all his resentments at the sleazy midnight world that he'd been suffering through. The men have come to her home, they tell her — to this farmhouse standing alone in an empty valley — because they've been tracking a suspect in the brutal sex murder of a young woman whose body was left in the snow. And the suspect, all three characters and the audience understand immediately, is Lupino's younger brother, whose mental illness has led him to do things he's unable to comprehend. The second man is Ward Bond, the victim's father — a primal, Ahab-like force bent on revenge, who swears that he will be the one who will shoot the suspect dead.

As Ryan stands between them, he sees two competing visions of himself: his past, embodied by Bond's malignant rage, or his possible future, embodied in Lupino's timorousness and bound-less affection. Ryan becomes intrigued with Lupino — both as person and as idea — as I did as well. It is in the middle of this snowbound valley, a landscape of de Chirico-esque solitude and estrangement, where I felt my own inner conflicts surge to the fore. In that darkened farmhouse standing alone in that rocky plain, Ray began to construct a parable about the conflict between the primitive craving for retribution and the higher calling of unconditional love.

In the very center of her living room stands — incongruously and inexplicably — a lacquered tree trunk. It was a gift, we learn, from her brother: a work of art he made for her to help guide her through her home, a symbol of life, even though it is already dead. Ryan watches her — as I did — as she carries her taut frame gingerly through her living room, moving half-step by half-step, by touch from one landmark to another — setting her fingers on the back of a chair, then two steps over to the tree in the center of the room, then one step forward and to the left where she reaches a few fingers ritualistically above her head to brush the ivy that hangs above the doorway. Her posture is stiff and pre-cise, as if she knows that she is modelling a series of poses — not for them but for herself — because she knows that her precision is her means of making this physical space navigable, which is a means of constructing both a psyche and a home that feel safe.

She tells Ryan that because of her blindness she has to trust everyone. But her posture tells us quite the opposite: her brittle inelasticity reveals her caution, her hesitancy, her need to make a protective shell of her own body. And Ryan, who has made a protective shell of his brutality and vengeance, is her very inverse; in his loneliness and his need, he is her mirror image. So the question that Ray has framed for us is, through her vulner-ability and her trust, her compassion and her love, is it possible for him — or for anyone — to be redeemed?

The climactic scene that unleashed such symphonic chords within me consists of just three shots in an indistinct bedroom. Bond had finally found Lupino's brother where she'd hid him on the farm and had chased him across a rocky outcropping

Fig. 2. Screenshot from *On Dangerous Ground* (dir. Nicholas Ray, 1952).

where the boy had fallen to his death. And now, the two men have brought the boy's body down from the mountain to lay to rest at a neighboring farm. Lupino has arrived and is sitting in the bedroom beside her brother's body so that she can say her final farewells. In the background, we can see through the window out in the frozen yard the group of men who'd hunted her brother down, while in the foreground Lupino, gazing off into nowhere, tenderly combs her brother's hair.

And then, the climactic close-up of her face. Her cheeks are already damp with drying tears reflected by the meager sun. The image is otherworldly. The background walls are gray — pure abstraction — as if she exists now only in symbolic space. Her face doesn't tremble. Her lower lip only hints at a quiver. Her eyes are barely wet. Her pupils reflect a light that can't possibly be there. Then, to signal that she's taking us with her, finally, into what will be the single most dramatic moment of the film, she raises her chin slightly (fig. 2).

"Father," she says quietly, subtly reinforcing the film's larger theme about the possibility of redemption, her voice hovering, unearthly. She looks up, searching, her face an infinitely subtle play of desperation, yearning, exhaustion, and fear: "Hear my prayer." And in that moment, I felt myself take a quick, panicked breath.

Lupino opens and closes her lips, as if she's unable to bring herself to speak — or as if her mind is hesitating over the inadequacy of the only words she can possibly summon. "Forgive him," she says, "as you've forgiven all your children who have sinned."[1]

In the brief sequence that follows, Ray positions us outside the house, in the snow, among the men who've been milling in the yard, so that Lupino — once forty feet tall in her climactic close-up — emerging out onto the porch of this unfamiliar, ramshackle dwelling, appears as a frail and inconsolable figure in the background, almost shrinking into the blandness of the image which is now dominated by Bond's henchmen in the foreground. They eye her warily, uneasy in their victory and in the death that they've brought to fruition, their shame now hanging in this frigid atmosphere like a miasma.

Lupino — who'd become the avatar of my voiceless optimism — takes one hesitant step after another, unable to see where she's going, reaching one hand against the façade to help her find her way. Her blindness now has become the cruel answer to her own prayer. She gazes blankly over the dim world before her. Her expression is lifeless because life has been torn from her. Her oversized dull-gray man's coat engulfs and enfeebles her. When she finally finds the end of the porch, she steadies herself with one hand against the wall, then slides one foot forward cautiously to find the edge. And Lupino, my emblem of hope, our vehicle for redemption, whose voice calls out to God though she knows she will hear no answer, lifts her arms shakily to balance herself, and then — without anyone's help because no one there even bothers to notice her — sets her foot down onto

---

1   Nicholas Ray, dir., *On Dangerous Ground* (1951; Warner Archive Collection, 2016), Blu-Ray disc, 1:10:45–1:13:09.

the barren earth to return once again and forever to the godless, ice-cold, and insensate world of men.

§

On some level I wasn't really searching at all. On some level, it felt quite the opposite; it felt, instead, as if something was searching through me. My capitulation to Tarr's exhaustive desolation and my emotional untethering under the spell of Lupino's disillusioned eyes were not conscious decisions; they were non-rational experiences. Aesthetic emotion emerges from the gut or from some unconscious kernel. When movies touched me, I knew I'd entered a zone where the conscious mind was no longer in control. I was driven — as we all are driven — by compulsions I could barely comprehend. We don't really choose art, after all. It feels, instead, that when we fall for a work of art, the external force of the object before us has come into contact with some starved void within that is reaching out, trying to latch on to a potential human feeling in order to let itself surface. It is, in other words, as if we ourselves are not even there. But this is one of the fundamental paradoxes of the aesthetic experience: we consciously use art as a means of fashioning our identities in contradistinction to the artless world that produced us, and yet, at the same time, this process of reimagination is simultaneously driven by forces beyond our conscious control.

When I sank into the experience of a movie — or perhaps, when it exerted its enigmatic hold over me — I was overcome, I discovered only years later, by that same feeling that Carl Jung described when we encounter an artwork that's deploying, or refiguring, what he called archetypes, the kinds of symbols that he suggested had become part of the storehouse of humanity's collective unconscious. And this was, he maintained, one of the primary purposes of art: to reconnect us with the myths of our ancestors and thus to our essential humanity. "The moment when this mythological situation reappears," he wrote, is always characterized by a peculiar emotional intensity; it is as though chords in us were struck that had never resounded before, or as though forces whose existence we never suspected were unloosed.... So it is not surprising that when an archetypal situation occurs we suddenly feel an extraordinary sense of release, as though transported, or caught up by an overwhelming power. At such moments we are no longer individuals, but the race; the voice of all mankind resounds in us.[2]

Jung thought that archetypes brought forth bursts of aesthetic intensity because they constituted a fundamental aspect of the mind. Every human being, he believed, innately shared a set of essential aesthetic concepts and desires in the same way that later theorists suggested that every human being innately shared the same fundamental building blocks of grammar — because they had been passed down to us, generation by generation, over the course of millennia. And Jung did not intend these notions about our lineage in a metaphorical sense. These aesthetic affinities, he maintained, lived — or perhaps hibernated — somewhere in the mind; they were, in fact, hardwired in the anatomical structure of the brain. Archetypes and artistic impulses were, in other words, genetically inherited. To feel an aesthetic resonance as I did when I came into contact with Béla Tarr or Ida Lupino, to Carl Jung's way of thinking, was to come into contact with my ancestral inheritance, to revivify a dormant cultural legacy.

The rationalist in me has looked askance at Jung ever since I first read him. His confidence in being able to ascertain the latent, invisible contents of our shared mental universe reminded me of a similar confidence I heard from pastors up in the pulpit when they tried to explain the nature of the Trinity. His ideas don't fall under the rubric of what we would normally consider

---

2   Carl Jung, "On the Relation of Analytical Psychology to Poetry," in *The Portable Jung,* ed. Joseph Campbell, trans. R.F.C. Hull (New York: Penguin Books, 1971), 320.

to be scientific or analytical knowledge. His vision of the mind is just as non-rational as the experiences he's trying to explain.

But the human animal harbors an innate need to engage in non-rational methods of cognition. We can productively entertain Jung's ideas about inherited aesthetic dispositions even if we don't necessarily believe — or even despite the fact that we positively do not believe — in them. In Western culture, we tend to think of religion as predicated upon belief, but we might consider it instead — as we do with Buddhism — as predicated chiefly upon practice. Neuroscientists have found that participating in religious ritual — a non-logical endeavor — quiets down the part of the brain that maintains the sense of self, which helps people forge bonds with others, thus solidifying functioning social networks. Cultural historians steeped in evolutionary theory, meanwhile, point out that organized religion came into being, not surprisingly, just when humans first began to settle down in agricultural communities and needed to nurture a sense of shared identity. Thus, non-rational thought and practice do serve a purpose.

Responding to art is a similarly non-rational enterprise. Our initial reaction is almost always instinctual and emotional. And obsessively going to the movies manifests many of the same qualities as going to church: with ritual regularity, cinephile devotees enter into the hushed environment of the theater as they would into the sanctified space of the nave, willingly subordinating their own desires to a superior force for the sake of their own enlightenment. Stripped of any belief system, a devotional practice like cinephilia is useful in the same way that religious ritual is. Many of us agnostic aesthetes raised in church understand art either instinctively or explicitly not as a rational antidote to religious non-rationality but as its non-religious but equally non-rational twin.

For a theorist interested in myths, it's no surprise that Jung ended up merely inventing other myths of his own: myths that we can deploy — if we choose — to explain ourselves back to ourselves. Perhaps it's only by embracing both rational and non-

rational modes of knowledge that we can reconcile the paradoxes of the aesthetic experience that define us.

So I had to admit, upon reflection, that Jung's analysis did
feel, instinctively, like the most discerning account I'd read about
the source of my most intense aesthetic experiences. When I
thought back to those moments in the movie theater when the
credits began to roll and I felt most rapturously destroyed, when
I first fell for movies like Rainer Werner Fassbinder's *Fear Eats
the Soul,* Robert Bresson's *Au Hasard Balthazar,* or Yasujiro Ozu's
Floating Weeds, it was clear that I had not made any conscious
decision to admire them. My enchantment at the transcendent
timbre of Lupino's voice and the polyphonic play of emotion
imbuing her statuesque face was an experience that issued forth,
unbidden, from some source invisible to me. I did not choose to
love her. I had, instead, been engulfed. Jancso's roving camera
and Welles's fervid audiovisual barrage had facilitated the awak-
ening of an entity that had been slumbering within — what Jung
called an "autonomous complex" — and which needed to unfurl
itself, stretch its limbs, and make itself known to me. The most
intense aesthetic experiences I had while sitting alone in a darkened theater felt, more often than not, like an act of submission
to an aspect of my persona that I had not yet had the acumen
to perceive.

These days, decades after I first fell for the films of directors
like Sergei Parajanov, Abbas Kiarostami, and Kenji Mizoguchi, I
don't go to the movies as obsessively as I did when I was young.
I've witnessed myself over the years slowly becoming middle-
aged. I'm in my fifties now, and I've changed, as we all do. Year
by year, decade by decade, I've slowly been easing out of what I
now think of, in retrospect, as the heroic age of cinephilia in my
twenties and thirties — or, perhaps, as merely a squandered age
of self-indulgent evasion. I've sensed myself drifting a bit, year
by year, from that youthful obsession that came to define me. I
don't go to the movies every day anymore; lately, it's been just
two or three times a week. But this languid evolution away from
the past hasn't been the product of any waning interest in the art
form. No. It has its source in the same force that made me go to

the movies in the first place — in the constant need to reimagine the self, in the constant need to dispatch the nagging suspicion that perhaps we have no interior core at all.

Now, I think, I'm able to look back at that earlier incarnation of myself with fresh eyes, and I've come to see that my compulsive moviegoing back then — or anyone's, at any time — has only a partial relationship with the love of movies or of art, with an embrace of entertainment for its own sake, or with a fierce engagement with any fictional characters or the worlds that they inhabit. Devotions like those fueled my moviegoing, for sure. Tarr's excremental skies and their incongruously empyrean allure, those grainy fatalistic film noir shadows, Lupino's husky timbre and omniscient gaze all struck chords, resonating with a deep-seeded spiritual disposition, as much as an aesthetic vision, that I can only articulate back to myself in retrospect: an embrace of the desire for spiritual redemption and its concomitant antinomic counterpart, the hopeless degradation of the skeptic. These were the values I'd absorbed in the anatomical structure of the brain, I've begun to tell myself, the virtues that coursed through my blood. And passions as elemental as these, passions that have been inherited, I've begun to suspect, were passions that logically looked backward, sensibilities that emanated from the depths of the past.

But I can see now the fundamental yet irresolvable tension that undergirds this notion about our response to art. On closer inspection, Jung hadn't described a single type of aesthetic reaction as at first it might have seemed. Rather, he'd described two possibly diametric phenomena in that moment of aesthetic intensity: our response felt, on the one hand, as if "caught up by an overwhelming power," but also, on the other hand, as an "extraordinary sense of release, as though transported."[3] The first is the experience of one autonomous mental complex taking control; the second, though, is the experience of another autonomous mental complex escaping that very control. I was drawn, after all, to Tarr's sepulchral skies but also to his orgi-

---

3   Ibid.

astic, liberated style, to Lupino's timorous fragility, but also to her compassionate resolve, to Ray's bleak interiors, but also to his desire for melodramatic redemption. My contradictory aesthetic responses made sense, though, because they echoed the two contrasting phenomena that Jung had described: one of restraint, the other of unfettering. On the one hand, our unconscious nurtures essential qualities of our character that need to surface: our most base instincts, the aspects of our personalities we've inherited from our ancestors. On the other hand, our mind simultaneously nurtures a countervailing force desperate to efface those very same embedded cultural attributes. But because these discordant phenomena are inextricably linked in a chain of cause and effect, they are, ultimately, one phenomenon, not two — of push and pull, tension and release — a circular dynamic that can never reach a satisfactory resolution.

We are defined, in other words, by our cultural past, but simultaneously by our need to break free from that past in order to construct a more functional present. Indeed, the specific qualities of our cultural inheritance produce the exact dimensions of their own undoing. Our most intense aesthetic experiences are governed by these irreconcilable internal conflicts, the paradox of our artistic taste and thus of our personality. Aesthetic emotions emerge, unbidden, from interior depths: the artistic experience releases our fundamental traits, but simultaneously releases those fundamental attributes' very negation, an antagonistic power that's developed its own strategies for unmasking and survival, a force bent on displacing its obdurate, antediluvian twin.

Our immediate, unthinking response to art is the physical trace of these primary dichotomies that structure our identities: the past that shaped our present and the future we aim to shape in its stead, our aesthetic inheritance and our individualist abnegation of that very bequest. My ostensible obsession with the art of film, it's come to seem to me, has merely been a means for these mental forces to make themselves known to me, a forum for my invisible desires to speak. The cinephile lifestyle is a product of an obsessive love of the movies, yes, but it's also the mental and physical manifestation of our innate need to unleash occulted personalities, our intrinsic imperative to forge a destiny of our own. We are not individuals, but merely mediums — or hosts — for an inborn conflict between autonomous complexes to play itself out, thus expanding our emotional and spiritual capaciousness so that this conflict can continue to breed.

Aesthetic emotion is thus founded upon a paradox. In one sense we find ourselves irresistibly drawn to art that speaks to our ingrained values: not just our surface characteristics, but the deeper, spiritual aspects of ourselves, the values we've inherited, materializing in our earliest years, inculcated by our parents, who absorbed them from their parents, who adopted them from their own. But at the same time, we are irresistibly drawn to the art we admire precisely because it helps us fashion our personalities in opposition to that very legacy. When we say, I like *this, this,* and *this,* but not *that, that,* or *that,* we are creating a unique self by distinguishing ourselves from others — most importantly, from those who had the greatest influence on us, the preceding generations who forged the culture we've imbibed since our youth. And we typically experience this push and pull most intensely at moments of aesthetic bliss. Indeed, aesthetic pleasure may be the most eloquent expression of these innate psychic conflicts struggling within. One of art's primary functions, then, must be to help us negotiate these antagonistic poles that organize our sense of self.

My love for Tarr's tar-black landscapes and depthless skies, then, was not a conscious decision that I made in a movie theater more than twenty years ago. His film made contact with the base yearnings that compel me — a longing for desolation and despair, discipline and self-denial, on the one hand, and a baroque, self-indulgent excess on the other, the uninhibited antagonist of that very self-denial, the ostentatious formalism that counteracts its essential bleakness, a flamboyant aesthetics that is the essence of hope, just as Lupino's unsullied empathy, too, was intrinsically connected to the frozen landscape that gave it birth. These are the twin poles of my cultural inherit-ance — the innate and irresolvable paradox of my aesthetics.

The images up on screen — piercing the darkness of the movie theater — have often played a more significant role in shaping my psyche than the events that make up what we might call real life. I would not be the first person to think that the material world is the world of illusions and that it is the immate-rial realm of the imagination instead that is the real. We often make meaning of our lives by reflecting on the fictional. We for-get our everyday experiences, we try to banish the traumatic, but we return again and again to certain aesthetic objects or experiences as a means of safeguarding ourselves.

To make sense of our lives, then, perhaps it's most rational to ignore the commonplace events that make up the bulk of our material existence and reflect instead on the stories and images that have most effectively penetrated us, those artistic encoun-ters that nurtured and brought to the surface the irreconcilable conflicts that have constituted our attempts to negotiate the self.

This memoiristic mode of reflection on life and identity is one of the most essential of our everyday mental operations. If a memoir is merely the more formal method of organizing a coherent narrative explanation of a life — a form of reckoning with the idea of the self — it does not necessarily need, then, to be an ordered recounting of past events. We are not solely — or, most interestingly — the facts that have happened to us. We are not our chronologies. We are just as much our desire to defy those events and that chronology, which often strike us, in ret-rospect, as not just random and meaningless, but as an insult to our conceptions of ourselves. It's true: those events may have happened, we grudgingly admit. But it might be more accurate to say that those events swirled around us. Yes, I may have done that and that. But that's not who I am. We are, as much, our need to counteract the explanatory narratives that time's arbi-trary unfolding has imposed upon us. We are, instead — we sometimes like to imagine — only the imagination, only will. We inhabit the sky as much as we tread this earth. We are mental forces which are merely capable, at their best, of casting shadows onto this material existence.

To be a faithful rendition of a life and of an identity, then, a memoir might as well be an exploration of the unconscious forces of the past and future that coordinate our character, an examination of the fundamental paradox of the self — in my case, of the antipodes of desolation and redemption I like to imagine have been bequeathed to me by powers that preceded my existence. But the unconscious is evanescent and inscrutable, hidden from our own intelligence; it can only disclose itself through the oneiric logic of misdirection and disorientation. In this sense, a truly memoiristic understanding of one's life might make most sense when it takes on the forms of the cinema itself: a collection of discordant images, fragments of feelings, and disjointed narratives that avoid resolution. We might, most fruitfully, then, attempt to find the essence of identity in the surge and flow of the aesthetic experience itself.

2

Frontier Images :: Myths of the Self

I can see the image — and I can hear it — though it plays out only in my imagination. The camera tracks forward in a point-of-view-shot, the field of vision seemingly nothing but color: the gold and cream and olive greens of tall grass oscillating across the screen to make an unceasing sound — a sibilant rustle or a swish — in front of a sky so seized by the sun that it's no longer blue but pure light, an almost blinding sheen, with the barely visible trace of clouds in their slow drift the only thing to remind us that this sky is more than just an emptiness, but perhaps even an entity, an agent with intention, and that the land has agency, too, so that these endless waves of tall grass are the earth's attempt to announce its feeble existence against the infinite disinterest of the heavens. And it feels like we're announcing our own existence as well, pushing forward through a swaying field, which appears now like the rhyming echo of the swelling ocean that brought us here, as if we've stepped ashore onto this plain, what appears to us as an unpeopled world. Then finally, in the second shot, from the reverse angle, we see ourselves for the first time: a stocky, bearded man in a woolen coat and straw hat strides through the grass that comes up above his waist and moves past the camera into off-screen space, a nine-year old boy trailing a few feet behind, and behind him a pair of oxen pulling a wagon

with creaking wooden wheels where an older woman in a ker-
chief sits, slouching forward on a plank, weary-eyed, staring
vacantly into the quivering, trampled grass, a small girl beside
her resting her head against her mother's lap. The wagon is piled
high with blankets, sheepskins, an enormous wooden chest, a
plow, scythes and hoes, a sickle sticking out over the wagon's
edge, and trailing behind them all, tethered to the wagon by a
slack rope, one skinny cow. In the third shot, a backward-track-
ing close-up of the bearded man, his eyes scan left to right, right
to left, searching, searching the horizon for anything other than
this endless expansion, this unrelenting undulation of the land,
this constant brushing of the wind in the grass made more con-
spicuous because of the absence of crickets or birds or wind in
any trees because there are no trees. And then, in the fourth
shot, from a bird's-eye view, this scraggly line of a family, the
wagon, and the cow continues on through the vast image of gold
and cream and olive green, as if there is nothing but this tall
grass, as if there is nothing but this swirling mass of color and
this swirling sound. And as the camera pulls farther and farther
away, the grass loses its shape, becomes nothing but a diminish-
ing golden cream, and we understand that they are lost, wandering through this color which is a landscape like an ocean.

The opening sequence of this movie has planted itself so
firmly and so vividly in my memory because on the one hand, it
resonates with the temperate vision of my identity that I like to
believe I've inherited from my Scandinavian immigrant ancestors, and on the other hand because, surprisingly, it isn't real.
These four shots — perhaps two minutes of screen time — make
up the first scene in a film that doesn't exist, but which I've been
imagining for almost two decades now: an adaptation of Ole
Edvard Rølvaag's novel *Giants in the Earth,* the great saga of the
Norwegian-American immigrant experience, which follows a
handful of settler families who build their first homes and their
first farms in the eastern prairies of the Dakota Territory in the
1870s, a region that then marked America's western frontier.
Many of my ancestors came from Norway — and Germany, Denmark, and Sweden, too — to settle in the Dakotas in the 1870s

and 1880s as well, and like the characters in Rølvaag's book, the first generation struggled as farmers, but eventually managed to build a life for themselves and their children. They constructed communities out on the prairie where the church stood as the tangible sign that they'd advanced beyond their earlier, more primitive way of life, so that faith became fundamental to the next generation's conception of its cultural ascendancy. When I first read the novel, I felt a surge of recognition: their story was my story, my soul seemed to be telling me, despite the obvious fact that my life was nothing like theirs at all. I embraced this novel as a meaningful version of the origin story of my family — and thus of myself — knowing full well that my embrace was an arbitrary means of mythmaking. The understanding of the self, after all, is a fictive act.

There are other movies, most of them real, that resonate with me for similar reasons. Austere, Scandinavian films about stoic characters undergoing a crisis of faith, in particular — like films by Ingmar Bergman and Jan Troell — have always struck a chord, just as Carl Jung argued that our inherited artistic values do, as if they're releasing pent-up memories: visions of spare wooden churches standing alone in the middle of a prairie I used to glimpse through a car window when I was young, or of my grandfather, the Lutheran pastor, standing aloft in the pulpit wearing a brightly colored stole over his pure white vestment and speaking softly in measured tones as he fixed his eyes on some indefinable presence off beyond the reach of his parishioners. My mind had kept these images in check because, back when I was 16, I'd made the decision to abandon the Lutheran faith that my ancestors had followed for hundreds of years. It was a means of forging a new future for myself by differentiating me from the path that my parents and their parents had shaped. But these conscious decisions always carry within them a paradox — because, as they say, you can leave the church, but the church doesn't leave you. Any attempt to shed the past may just push it deeper into the unconscious, where it then finds ways to make its presence known in stranger, more unruly manifestations. Dreaming up an imaginary movie was a way of consciously shaping a future, but the fact that I imagined a film about my ancestors was a sign of how difficult it is to escape the past.

There's one image, especially, I keep returning to, that keeps inspiring a Jungian resonance: an early scene from *Ordet,* a Danish film from 1954 directed by Carl Theodor Dreyer, whose title translates simply as *The Word.* The camera angles upward through tufts of tall grass at the edge of a dune where a timid figure, long-haired and scraggly-bearded, seems almost to be disappearing into the center of the frame, almost to be disappearing into his too-large coat. He gazes vacantly over the rolling expanse of his imaginary domain, what must be a landscape of sand dunes and beyond that perhaps an inestimable sea, fanning out invisibly to us in off-screen space. Though he's clearly the focus of the image, he's a mere speck beneath a boundless wash of sky that looms behind him. The black-and-white film stock is so monotonously gray I can feel the image's claustrophobic yearning, as if the colorlessness itself evinces the limited emotional range that the Danish landscape or the Lutheran faith has made available to this character — and to me.

And yet this color also renders the hidden depths I like to imagine constitute the Scandinavian soul, a drab monochrome that masks a vibrant abundance of color invisible to the casual gaze: this gray has hints of cream and ash, the diffuse wash of a watercolor's eggshell blue, and specks of a spiritual gloaming but also of promise and yearning. As the shot continues to unfurl, the wind swirling and dissipating on the soundtrack, the protagonist Johannes, whom we'd seen minutes earlier in the opening scene escaping from the spartan interior of his rustic family farm into this metaphorical void, lifts his arm listlessly and begins to speak in a disturbingly loud and unmodulated tone to an imagined crowd whose absence is the sign of his mental instability. "Woe unto you, hypocrites," he intones, "unto you, and you, and you. Woe unto you for your lack of faith! Woe unto you who do not believe in me, the risen Christ, who was sent to

Fig. 3. Screenshot from *Ordet* (dir. Carl Theodore Dreyer, 1955).

you by Him who made the heavens and the earth. Verily I say unto you, the day of judgment is at hand"[1] (fig. 3).

Ordet has burned itself so intensely into my unconscious because its central conflict between two forms of religious devotion — an ardent self-restraint and a liberating spiritual fervor — seems so central to my own background as well. The story focuses on a devout farming family who struggle to deal with one son whose mental illness has led him to the sacrilegious idea that he is Jesus Christ, and with another son who's announced his engagement to a girl from a family that belongs to a schismatic sect. In Denmark at that time of the story, there was a rift in the Lutheran faith between those like the protagonist's family, who remained committed to the state-sponsored church, and others who embraced a new movement that challenged the authority of the state, emphasizing the ability of lay preachers and the common people to forge their own passion-

---

1   Carl Theodor Dreyer, dir., *Ordet* (Palladium Film, 1955; Criterion Collection, 2015), Blu-Ray disc, 4:19–6:29.

ately intimate relationship with God. And yet, as Dreyer makes clear, despite their intense embrace of faith, both families, and thus both of the competing sects, ignore or disparage Johannes even though — or rather, precisely because — he spends the entire film uttering the exact words of Jesus.

Because of Dreyer's obsessiveness, the image itself always becomes the bearer of his convictions, a vision that is ultimately as fatalistic as it is miraculous. Its insistent asceticism, its endless fascination with the minute gradations of the gray sky and the sound of wind, its seeming disinterest in the miniscule human figures that now and then dot the empty, windblown landscape, all help to shape a world in which the characters' spiritual aspirations are constrained by their environment, because only landscapes, after all — not interiors — can adequately emphasize the idea of isolation. But the film's enervated atmosphere is continually pierced by the wind as much as it is by theological disputes: sheets and shirts hanging from the clothesline in the far distance dance about as if animated by some invisible force that might disturb the monotony of life on the farm, and yet the sheets and shirts are so small and so distant that many viewers might not even notice them. The wind whipping itself into this boundless void, then, hints at Dreyer's primary themes: because of the family's inner restraint, the few emotions that do manage to reveal themselves flare up like fissures in the atmosphere. The ostentatious austerity of the image, of grays saturated with sterility, is the very cause of the yearning to escape this community's constraints, but it is also the force that limits that yearning, that limits the possibilities of the miraculous by bounding God's love for humanity in a world that is still — and will always be — devoid of color and ornamentation.

Dreyer brings his religious conflicts to a head by bringing death to the family, when Johannes's sister-in-law Inger dies unexpectedly in childbirth near the end of the film. The tragedy, ironically, enables everyone to see clearly for the first time how their theological disputes have prevented them from living lives inspired by Christ's example. Dreyer stages the film's climactic scene as Inger's body lies in state. In a room as resolutely monochrome as the sky has appeared throughout the film, Johannes enters to pay his respects, making everyone else uneasy, an encounter that we understand immediately will bring the film to its culmination.

Dreyer casts onto the pale, desiccated walls only a feeble glow that emphasizes the space's signifying flatness rather than its realistic three-dimensionality. The furniture, too, is spare: a wooden pendulum clock hangs in the center of one wall, and a few stiff wooden chairs are scattered across the floor. The men wear black suits, white shirts, and black bow ties, and sit like islands alone in opposite corners. In her coffin in the center of the room, Inger, laid out in a pure white dress against a pure white pillow, looks as perfect and as chilling as a painting. Johannes, clear-eyed now for the first time in the film, tells his father that he's regained his wits. And yet, his discrepancy with the family is still quite clear; unlike everyone else, he wears tan slacks and a tan sweater. He's earthier, less constrained by their culture's expectations, but still just as muted and plain.

Eventually, the scene's slow crawl builds to the moment we've sensed for a long time was inevitable, the climactic challenge of Johannes's sacrilegious claim that he speaks with the voice of God himself. The only person in the room who pays him any mind is the dead woman's little daughter, who comes to hold his hand in an innocent act of solidarity. Only she who is ignorant, it seems, can actually have the faith that Jesus has required of us.

In that moment, Johannes looks calmly, directly into the girl's eyes. Just as calmly, he asks her if she believes that he has the power to accomplish this momentous task. Without flinching, she answers, "Yes."

And in a voice that's utterly serene but utterly resolute, he informs her that when he pronounces the name of Jesus Christ, her mother will rise from the dead.

Then, standing before his sister-in-law's lifeless body, he commits either the single most blasphemous act or the ultimate fulfillment of religious conviction as he begins to speak. Gazing off into the heavens, his voice takes on the same otherworldly monotone he's used before when he's seemed most unstable.

And at this moment, the film begins to work on multiple levels, since Johannes is not just blaspheming against the Christian standards of his community and against the grief of every character in the room, but Dreyer himself is blaspheming as well against the acceptable bounds of the cinema, the paradigmatic medium of the secular age. "Jesus Christ," Johannes intones, "if it is possible, then give her leave to come back to life, give me the Word, the Word that can make the dead come to life. Inger, in the name of Jesus Christ, I bid thee… rise."[2]

The first time I saw *Ordet,* my chest heaved in anticipation at this moment, a few charged, timeless seconds, waiting anxiously for God knows what, shocked at myself that I could be so deeply moved by something so banal as the yearning for the miraculous. And then I realized that I'd heard myself gasp out loud. Because there before me, larger than life on screen, laid out in her coffin in a pure white dress against a pure white pillow, her hands clasped gently on her stomach, the dead woman's fingers twitched, then moved. Then, slowly, she unclasped her hands, and, at the sound of her husband's voice, opened her eyes.

§

I remember Grandma Ina taking the family photo albums out of the sideboard and sitting down beside me on the sofa. The moment was always charged. She and I were performing a ritual that we repeated every summer. We looked out through a window at a stand of birch trees, ensconced in a little house in the woods overlooking a lake in northern Minnesota. The album had a leather cover. When she opened it, it made a sound. As if air had been trapped in a dark well since forever. The pages were thick, almost turning yellow from age, and they creaked when she turned them. Like the flutter of leaves in the distance. Each page had three or four black and white photographs of people I didn't recognize, but who, she told me in a voice suffused with a nonchalant resolution, were my relatives. The photographs

---

2 Ibid., 1:56:20–2:04:40.

Fig. 4. The family of Stener Hilde and Gertrude Johnson Hilde. Courtesy of the author.

didn't have captions. Words, after all, would have denied her the opportunity of explaining them to me.

"This," she would say, "is your great-grandfather Stener Hilde. He was born in Norway in 1862. This is your great-grandmother Gertrude Johnson Hilde. Her parents came from Norway, but she was born in Iowa in 1873." Stener sits upright in a pin-striped suit, with a stiff, tall, white collar, hair parted perfectly down the middle, staring intently into the camera, clearly the center around which his wife and eight children orbit. His mustache — the only authentic aspect of this image, I suspect — appeared to my younger self as operatically oversized as the past itself. His wife, Gertrude, wearing the same black dress as her daughters who stand beside her, holds a baby in her lap — my great-aunt Clara, Grandma informs me — whose white dress reflected the flash of the photographer's lights so brightly she's become just a chalky blur, a smudged blaze, as if a German Expressionist had dipped his paintbrush into my family's history to introduce his idea of an angel (fig. 4).

I remember Grandma Alice taking the family photo albums out of a wooden cabinet that she called a "credenza." She sat beside me on a sofa with the leather-bound book on her lap as she did every summer when we came to visit, as if we were performing a ritual. We sat together in a six-story apartment building in Grand Forks, North Dakota. When she opened the book, it made a sound. A pent-up release, like the breath of ghosts. Each page had three or four black and white photographs protected by a plastic sheet. The pages were so thick, they creaked when she turned them. Like a rustling tree in the distance. The photographs didn't have captions. That would have denied her the opportunity of explaining them to me.

"This," she would say, "is your great-great-grandfather John Caspar Hummel and your great-great-grandmother Louise Schwandt Hummel. He was born in Bavaria in 1865. She was born in Prussia in 1872. He was a Lutheran pastor and her family were parishioners in his church in Big Stone City, South Dakota, before they moved up to Litchville, North Dakota, a few years later. This is their wedding photo from 1892." My great-great-grandparents stand a foot apart from each other. They do not touch. They do not smile. They do not look each other in the eye. His beard is orotund, providential. His black suitcoat reaches to his knees. Her white dress is as rigid as a plate of armor, though she wears a headband of fresh flowers in her hair. They gaze intently into the camera with all the seriousness they can muster because they know that they are gazing into the nexus of the future for the benefit of their descendants whom they will never know.

One of photography's principal tasks ever since its invention has been to commemorate the family. And since the nineteenth century, the family photo album has become the primary means of making meaning of our heredity. Susan Sontag suggested that photography took up this mission because it came into being at a time and place when conceptions of kinship were undergoing tectonic shifts. "As that claustrophobic unit, the nuclear family," she wrote, "was being carved out of a much larger family aggregate, photography came along to memorialize, to restate symbolically, the imperiled continuity and vanishing extendedness of family life."[3] People invented the photo album to stave off the demise of the traditional family; they deployed the new technology, ironically, in order to protect themselves from modernity.

And yet Sontag's most counterintuitive insight was to uncover the unexpected connections between the family photo album and tourism. People take photographs on vacation, she suggests, for much the same reasons that they collect pictures of long-dead relatives. By taking snapshots of themselves at Mount Rushmore, on a beach in Hawai'i, or on top of the Empire State Building, tourists are trying to demonstrate to their future selves that these moments were more significant than they actually felt at the time; they're validating actual experience by embalming it in an image, transforming the ephemeral into the permanent. And by returning to that image over the years, people revive their memories as a way of legitimizing their identities. *I was there. I did this. I am the type of person who had this adventure, felt this authentic joy.*

People use pictures of their family, surprisingly, for much the same purpose. We don't look at old pictures to memorialize our antecedents, but to make sense of our own identities in the present. Looking at old photos is a way of visiting and putting our stamp on a foreign land; it's a means of affirming our own lives by making our links to the past feel more significant than we actually feel in our everyday lives. And we need to use them this way precisely because contemporary life is so unstable, so threatening. Sontag wrote that "as photographs give people an imaginary possession of a past that is unreal, they also help people take possession of space in which they are insecure."[4] So we often use photographs not so much as historical documents or as aids to visual perception but as a form of therapy, just as my intensive cinephilia has always functioned as a mode of self-interpretation. And yet, photography's purportedly ameliorative function will always remain ultimately incomplete because

3   Susan Sontag, "In Plato's Cave," in *On Photography* (New York: Picador/ Farrar Strauss Giroux, 1973), 9.

4   Ibid.

photographs cannot suture the chasms of time and space on their own. As Sontag repeatedly insisted, photographs can never offer up any meaning by themselves. Only language — captions, essays, someone's spoken explanations — can provide us with any worthwhile knowledge about the meaning of a photographic image.

But when I look at pictures from the old family albums today, there are no captions accompanying them. There is no text to give them meaning. Both my grandmother Ina and my grandmother Alice are long dead. These photographs can't speak on their own. Now, generations after their owners have passed on, family photo albums have begun to function differently than they were originally intended to because the people who were supposed to provide their meaning by explaining them are no longer with me. But these images, like all images, still yearn for explication. Today, though, the only means we have of explaining them to ourselves is with the power of the imagination. In the absence of captions, our unconscious must necessarily dream.

§

My first ancestors to land in America, my great-great-great-grandparents Andreas and Olea Lundene, came from Norway in 1850 to Springdale, Wisconsin, which by that time had become the geographical center of the first wave of Norwegian immigrants to settle in America. Every other line of my ancestors arrived from that point on, from Norway, Sweden, Denmark, and Germany, first the Lundenes, then the Jacobsons, the Johnsons, the Jeglums, the Hildes, the Jorgensons, the Melbys, the Ringdahls, the Flugekvams, the Bubachs, the Dibberns, the Stelcks, the Schwandts, and finally my great-great grandfather John Caspar Hummel, from whom I get my middle name, who arrived on these shores in 1886. They settled first in Wisconsin, Iowa, Minnesota, and the Dakota Territory. They had been farmers in the old country and they became farmers once again. They raised their children on farms and their children became farmers just like them. Then, from 1870 to 1910, a second wave of resettlement commenced — this time an internal migration made possible because of the defeat and forced relocation of the Ojibwe, the seven bands of the Sioux, the Mandan, the Hidatsa, and the Arikara on the frontier[5] — as every strand of my family continued to gravitate westward, generation by generation, until most of them found themselves living on farms along the eastern edge of North Dakota, the Norwegian-American heartland, where my grandparents' generation was born and raised. And my grandparents' generation in turn began a third wave of migration, moving this time from the farm into town, embracing the way of life that the rest of their descendants, including me, have carried on to this day. My parents were the products of this final phase, born in 1947 in Grand Forks, North Dakota, which had back then a population of 25,000, making it the biggest metropolis, the throbbing nexus of civilization, for almost a hundred miles around.

One reason it became so easy for me to idealize the lives of settlers on the Plains — like the characters in *Giants in the Earth* — was because even by the time my parents were born, life on the farm had already ceased to exist, taking on the patina of a mythic age. My grandparents grew up on 160-acre tracts, legacies of the Homestead Act, in some of the most sparsely populated counties in the nation, where towns of only a few hundred people sprouted up here and there every dozen miles

---

5 Indigenous naming conventions are currently in flux. Throughout the book, I've tried to refer to people by the names that the majority of those communities have chosen for themselves. Historian Pekka Hämäläinen explains in *Lakota America* why he uses the term "Sioux": "Although problematic, 'Sioux' remains the most common English term used by Lakotas and non-Natives alike. And many modern Lakota *oyates* identify themselves as Sioux tribes." Hämäläinen notes that the term "Očhéthi Šakówiŋ" technically refers only to the seven tribes known as the "Seven Council Fires," whereas four other eastern "Dakota" tribes sometimes use the term "Sioux" as well, thus the term "Sioux" is a bit more expansive relative to the larger culture I'm usually referring to. See Pekka Hämäläinen, *Lakota America: A New History of Indigenous Power* (New Haven: Yale University Press, 2019), ix.

or so. But the years of my grandparents' childhood marked both the climax and the final act of five decades of explosive growth in North Dakota: from 1880 — just after the US cavalry had finally defeated the Lakota and the federal government had relocated them and every other local indigenous tribe onto reservations — to 1930, when my grandparents still lived with their parents on the farm, the state's population surged from 37,000 to 680,000.

But the Great Depression marked the end of the era when the descendants of these European settlers took up the life of farmers themselves. After 1930, the state's population — now almost exclusively white — remained roughly the same for the next eighty years while the population of the country as a whole almost tripled. Henry Ford's tractors and combine harvesters, the consolidation of smaller family farms by larger corporations, and the Dust Bowl of the 1930s all brought an end to the family farm. The number of Americans who worked in agriculture dropped from 40% in 1900 to 12% in 1950,[6] and my family exemplified that transition. My four grandparents were all born on farms between 1907 and 1922. But of the 27 children born to their families on the farm in that generation, not a single one went on to live on a farm themselves: by 1940, every single one of those children had abandoned that way of life and moved on. It was their generation that marked the third wave of migration — not so much geographical as it was cultural, economic, and psychological — moving from the rural to the metropolitan milieu. The men took office jobs and the women became homemakers. They settled down in wooden houses with indoor plumbing and backyards and front lawns that faced paved sidewalks and streets. And in doing so, they forever cemented the tales — and the cultural ethos — of their parents' generation as the authentic experience of idealized hardship they'd pass on to their own children and grandchildren, creating for me the

---

6   *Historical Statistics of the United States, Colonial Times to 1970, Part 1* (Washington, DC: United States Bureau of the Census, 1975), 126–27.

notions about ethnic origins I saw reflected back to me in Rølvaag's *Giants in the Earth*.

In the oldest family photo I can find, taken in 1867, my greatgreat-great-grandparents Andreas and Olea Lundene — my first ancestors, back in 1850, to set foot on American shores — sit with their eight children. They look dour, stern, joyless, sexless, and rigid. It's not just the fear of God but an anger at life itself that I see in their faces. Andreas Lundene and the boys all wear black suits with stiff white collars and black bow ties that hang loosely across their chests. Their hair is parted perfectly on the left, fixed in place and shiny with Macassar oil. The boys look vacant, stupid, afraid. Olea Lundene and the girls all wear black dresses with stiff white collars, their straight, flat hair parted perfectly in the middle. My great-great-great-grandmother wears a bonnet. The oldest boy and girl, standing in the back, clasp their hands together as if they're about to curtsy before a queen. The girls look primal, animalistic, afraid.

In a photo from 1896, my great-great grandparents Moses and Zahanna Flugekvam sit with their nine children, who stare at the camera bug-eyed. The boys each wear the same grey suit with the same black tie. The girls each wear the same black dress with the same white collar. My great-great grandfather has the foot-long, forked beard of a Biblical prophet and a mustache that grows over his mouth. My great-great-grandmother has a plasticine expression, as if she were an icon carved out of soap. The family looks haunted and dour and sexless and afraid.

These images, I know, are not windows into the truth of my origins; they are fabrications, imaginative performances of the self. My ancestors were taking advantage of the new technology of photography as a ritualistic procedure to stage an idea of themselves that they could bequeath to the future — an attempt in their own time equal to my own attempt in the present to fashion a new identity for themselves. These efforts, though, bear within them the paradox of self-invention. From one perspective, these families were trying to eradicate the links across time by inventing these idealized images of themselves in the present in order to differentiate themselves from their own even more hardscrabble predecessors who'd first arrived in America. But seen from another angle, because they were designing the idea of themselves in these photographs for the benefit of their own descendants who would follow — transforming their own fictive present into the future's past precisely so that the future would then feel a link with its own predecessors — my ancestors were not erasing, but inevitably reinforcing the ineradicable links across time. And yet as strong as these bonds will be, they will always be, by their very nature, constructed upon an illusory representation.

The fact that every photograph was an economic product of its specific time and cultural milieu lays bare how consciously and meticulously previous generations were inventing these images and these ideas of themselves. Back in the nineteenth century, a photograph was an expensive occasion. When my great-great-grandparents John Caspar and Louise Hummel took their wedding photograph in 1892, they most likely had to dip in to their savings or borrow money from their parents, make an appointment weeks in advance, and travel dozens of miles to another town. When my great-grandparents Stener and Gertrude Hilde took their family photograph in 1909, they had to buy or mend and wash the finest set of clothes for every member of the family. They had to find a way to transport every single one of those family members at the same time into town, maybe even several towns over, back before anyone yet owned an automobile.

These families knew that they could afford to take only one or two photographs of themselves over the course of their lives — usually, it seems, at a wedding before they had children or once they assumed that they'd finished having children — so they carefully orchestrated these pictures of themselves. Every single one of the people in these nineteenth-century images was living on a farm at the time the photo was taken, but not a single one of them looks like a farmer. Every family photograph is a staging of both shame and the particular aspirations that that type of shame engenders. These families designed these pictures to shroud their authentic selves and replace them with a romanticized vision. Every act of creation is always an act of negation. Every family photograph is both a curative and a wound.

Yet these invented ideals were not the product of a wholly autonomous imagination; they were, like all artworks, shaped by the technologies of their time. To produce these portraits, they had to gather in a photographer's studio and stand immobile in an uncomfortable act of endurance. The necessarily rigid formality of the era's mechanical image-making system shaped their aesthetic understanding of family. There were no casual photos from the nineteenth century, no everyday images, no snapshots. And so there was typically no humor, no quirkiness, no idiosyncrasy. It was as if the entire era denied itself the potential plenitude of its own personality. So my own notions that temperance and self-discipline comprise fundamental qualities of my own persona come as much from these photographed illusions as they do from a spartan religion or from the barren landscapes that infused my grandparents' childhoods. To the extent, then, that I've conceived of my own identity based on these family photo albums, I've crafted my sense of myself not only on a fabrication, but on the fabrication of a void, the carefully crafted camouflage of a psychic abyss.

Those moments when Grandma Ina or Grandma Alice pulled a photo album out from a sideboard or credenza were so psychically charged partly because there were so few family photographs that had survived. And this disintegration of our visual lineage has only deepened over the years. Those photo albums themselves, in fact, don't exist anymore. When my grandparents died, their children — my parents and aunts and uncles — split the photos up among themselves, dispersing images across state lines, disrupting memories, shutting down any sense of kinship, any notion of a web of connection among the next generation. So I had to track these images down myself, gathering digital files from here and there so that I could create a new image of my ancestry to replace the older image that my grandparents had invented for me when I was young. Surprisingly, though, given my grandparents' desire to pass on stories to the children in my generation, I've only been able to find eight photos of my ancestors from the nineteenth century, only eight photos that can explain myself back to myself by means of a link to the distant past.

And yet, my family's dismemberment of its own photographic history was not as surprising as at first it seemed. As much as we use photography, as Sontag suggests, to invent a fixed position for the past in order to stabilize our position in the present, we also have an equally powerful countervailing impulse that she leaves largely unexplored. The truth is that we often use these photographs in quite the opposite way: that is, we can also stabilize our position in the present by banishing these images of our ancestry from our consciousness.

The desire to look through the family photo album carries within it the same paradox that defines our aesthetic desires. On the one hand, we use the images of our family in the past to define ourselves; we want to know where we came from in order to know who we are. But on the other hand, we use the family photo album to invest our present with meaning by distinguishing ourselves from our ancestors, to draw lines between the present and the past. We can only articulate an identity, after all, by drawing distinctions between ourselves and others. The family photo album, then, speaks to me in the same way that movies do. I read into them as much as I read into any film. And experiencing them prompts the same types of aesthetic imaginings, inspired by the same conflicting unconscious desires. I see in these photographs the desolation of Béla Tarr's diseased skies, the tenderness of Ida Lupino's eyes, the redolent silences of Carl Theodor Dreyer's windswept landscapes, but also — though I'm reluctant to admit it — the same yearning for redemption that Johannes, the mad believer, embodies in his journey into his own psychic interior.

But this paradox can never be resolved. As much as I'm drawn into these images, I resist. These people made me, but they are not me, I say to myself when I flip through those eight images once again. I could not possibly have come from them.

I sit down at my laptop and study once more the photograph, from 1915, of my great-great-grandfather Moses Flugekvam.

And once again I feel like a tourist in an unfamiliar land. He was born in 1846 outside of a town called Jølster, near Norway's west coast, a land of mountains and glaciers, lakes and dramatic, fog-laden fjords. At the age of 36 he, along with his wife Zahanna Tollefsdottir and their children, emigrated to the United States where they settled on a farm in Walsh County, Dakota Terri-tory, on land that just decades earlier had been the center of the Lakota empire, a land of flat prairie as far as the eye could see. He seems distant, alien. And yet he's not that far from me: Grandma Ina knew him well. He was, after all, her own grandfa-ther; when she was a child, they lived on farms just a few miles apart. She visited with him all the time, sat beside him on a sofa when she was a little girl and listened to him tell stories about his own childhood back in the old country. She probably told me those same stories about him back when I was young and sat beside her on a sofa looking at this very image.

Moses Flugekvam's visage is both tender and grim. His hoary beard is bristly and overflowing; it reaches to his chest. His snow-white mustache, the size of an abalone shell, melds into his beard so seamlessly it seems as if he can have no mouth to speak with, a voiceless messenger, a statuesque token of another age. I gaze into his eyes. They are deep, like the Old Testament, like obsidian pools. But nothing can escape their gravitational pull. They cannot possibly speak to me as much as my soul wants them to. Nor can I possibly speak back to him (fig. 5).

§

I've imbued North Dakota with so much spiritual weight, ironi-cally, precisely because I've never lived there: its physical absence has been the surprising source of its metaphorical power. The need to fashion a mythic homeland has been with me ever since I was young, I think, because I was raised in Arizona, a state that seemed devoid of history. No one had any roots there. Even in grade school, most of my classmates had been born in some other state. The desert landscape around me was so different from the image of America I saw on TV and read about in books

Fig. 5. Moses Flugekvam. Courtesy of the author.

at school, I might as well have lived on the moon. Phoenix, in fact, hadn't existed just one hundred years before I moved there. It had emerged suddenly in the early twentieth century along the banks of the Salt River on the northern edge of the Sonoran Desert, where for most of the summer the temperature hovered over 100 degrees, a land so arid it was difficult to imagine, as child, why anyone would want to live there — or how anyone could. It was only decades later, as an adult living on the other side of the continent, that I learned about the Akimel O'odham who had lived there for hundreds of years before the arrival of the Americans, of the Hohokam culture that had preceded them for a thousand years, and of the other cultures that had thrived in the valley for thousands of years before that.[7]

Yet the desert's forbidding appearance was the source of a surprisingly fertile creativity that functioned for American newcomers in the late twentieth century as North Dakota had for the late nineteenth: a vanquished, allegedly emptied landscape opened up for white settlers, a geographic tabula rasa — or so they conveniently convinced themselves — where emigrants could re-imagine themselves anew. When I was growing up, almost every building I ever came across — every shopping center and office park, every school, and every friend's home — hadn't been there even thirty years earlier. It was a land of parking lots and six-lane streets, highway overpasses and convenience store drive-throughs, where earlier arrivals had torn up the vibrant Sonoran flora and replaced it with asphalt and patchy yards of faded Bermuda grass.

But this new artificial landscape was a reminder, for those who wished to see, of the limits of our imagination, the visible sign that our ability to fashion a new future will inevitably be bound up in and constrained by the past. The new immigrants had left their old lives behind only to make their new lives a

---

7   Suzanne K. Fish and Paul R. Fish, eds., *The Hohokam Millennium* (Santa Fe: School for Advanced Research Press, 2007), and David H. DeJong, *Diverting the Gila: The Pima Indians and the Florence-Casa Grande Project, 1916–1928* (Tucson: University of Arizona Press, 2021), 18–40.

mirror image of the world that they'd so eagerly abandoned, transforming the desert into a horticultural replica of the Midwest. If the innate need to reinvent ourselves is always conjoined with its opposite disposition, the desire to cling to our origins, then Phoenix, with its mulberry trees and sprinkler systems and olive-green lawns, is the quintessential urban manifestation of this irresolvable tension.

The Sonoran Desert, though — or what little remained of it — was much more beautiful than the civilization the colonizers had replaced it with. Back then, I could see it only in patches — in an occasional front yard in the neighborhood, in the median of the road, or on a school trip to the botanic garden where the lush, profuse colors of the otherworldly bushes and science-fiction trees always made me wonder why the yards and streets and parks that surrounded me everywhere else in the city seemed so lifeless and dull.

The desert was a reminder of an even greater force than the collective imagination. The mountains and cliffs and river valleys, the cactus and the creosote, the lupines and thistle and marigolds that flowered, miraculously, every year as a proclamation of teeming life in opposition to the unrelenting heat and suffocating aridity had all been there for thousands of years before white people had entered the valley — before even the Akimel O'odham and their predecessors had been there — before human beings had invented the cinema or the printing press or cave paintings, before human beings had entered the Western Hemisphere, before human beings had even learned to speak. Landscapes are the emblem of geological time, a reminder of humanity's ultimate ephemerality, and thus a constant critique — if we care to notice — of our obsession with our own individuality.

People think of the desert as barren, but the land — when you could catch a glimpse of it — was flush with luxuriant vegetation set against a majestic backdrop: an undulating golden earth pierced here and there by purple and orange spires of rock. Once you got out of the city, you could see greenery everywhere: prickly-pear cactuses, with cascading clusters of oval, plate-sized, olive-green pads that grew out of and on top of each other, flecked with inch-long thorns and crowned with hand-fuls of hot-pink, pear-shaped fruit; barrel cactuses, sometimes a robust, foot-tall ball of spiky yellow needles, sometimes a pale, fuzzy cylinder jutting right up to your knee, lined with orange spines whose bright magenta and yellow flowers bloomed late in summer; cholla cactuses, agglomerations of twisting, inter-laced lime-green arms so skinny they looked like links of sau-sages covered with wisps of an old man's beard of soft downy needles; palo verde trees like the one that towered over our backyard where we struggled to grow even the scruffiest tufts of grass, their skinny, creased, cross-hatched trunks, and their bent, meandering branches a mix of mantis green and a baby blue so pale the trees appeared as pastel streaks fading into a distant canvas, their branches covered not with leaves but with packs of foot-long needles that fell and coated the ground which I'd rake up once a month into little heaps like golden haystacks before I'd carry them out to the dumpster in the alley; and oco-tillo bushes, clutches of spine-covered whips reaching out eight feet from the ground, dangling and swaying with purplish red flowers over the earth. If ever we went on hikes out into the desert we'd finally see animal life — wrens and owls and wood-peckers who made their homes inside the statuesque arms of saguaros; roadrunners that darted here and there between stands of creosote bushes; quails with royal black plumes that leaped up in sudden arcs of flight in threes and fours above our heads; hawks that floated above the desert for hours on end in lazy circles; the stout, hairy pigs known as javelinas with their sloping snouts and triangular profiles; sidewinder rattlesnakes; diamondbacks; kingsnakes; pencil-thin garter snakes; the four-legged, splotchy, multi-colored venomous lizard known as the Gila monster; jackrabbits that darted in and out of view between mesquite trees; tarantulas and scorpions and black widow spi-ders with red hourglass abdomens; and my favorite, the corpu-lent, rust-brown and striped-tailed, four-foot-long, fur-covered creature that slept during the hottest stretches of the afternoon in the branches of the palo verde like a giant, drunken raccoon, the creature with the impossibly mellifluous name of the coati-mundi.

But all of this had been concealed from me. The new emigrants of the late twentieth century hadn't just tried to refashion their environment by importing mulberry trees and oleander bushes and acres of Bermuda grass; they had tried to erase the earth's very spirit, its character and idiosyncrasy. They had tried to control the land when they could have tried, instead, to free themselves by submitting to the land's expansiveness and expressivity. But their vision of control was ultimately delimited by the paucity of human perception. The most recent human interlopers in the desert, with their circumscribed faculties, couldn't conceive of time as anything other than a straight line that connected the present with its immediately preceding and immediately succeeding generations.

But the pock-marked purple rocks on the mountain peaks surrounding the valley reveal another way of looking at things: the epic sprawl and endurance of the land and the unending reaches of the sky suggest that time's infinitude cannot be contained on a mere line; the meager linkage between one human generation and the next pales in comparison to the earth's vast evolutionary history. These new settlers' attempt to shape their future selves by reshaping the desert was ultimately a failure, then, because they failed to comprehend time's geological and celestial reach, and thus they failed to productively inhabit time's non-linearity.

If we cannot reimagine ourselves without unconsciously drawing on our own past and our own genealogy, we cannot reimagine ourselves unless we consciously reckon with the boundless history of the earth and of the heavens. The land and the sky are both eternity's herald and sentinel, simultaneously counteracting and inspiring the human mind's infinitesimal endeavors to comprehend and thus to become one with them.

§

Fig. 6. Photograph of the Sonoran Desert from a postcard attributed to Bob Petley (1912–2006).

I've never lived in North Dakota, haven't spent any time there in almost forty years, and have never visited any of the homes where my parents or their parents were raised, but every summer before I turned twelve, my family drove through that part of the country that once marked the western frontier to visit my grandparents. So when I look at photographs today of stretches of North Dakota highways, the images of those flat landscapes of shorn fields revive something within me: the vibration of unconscious chords, dormant psychic states set adrift. Over the last few years, I've found myself returning again and again to look at images on Google Maps of the long, empty highways running through the farmlands where my parents, grandparents, great-grandparents, and great-great-grandparents made their homes. I've used these pictures, their monumental blandness, their grandiloquent vacuousness, as a way to think about where I came from and who I am, as if the land itself — or more precisely, the photographic reproductions of the land — might reveal to me something of the emotional tenor of my ancestors' lives in the past, of their very spirit, from which I've inherited, I like to imagine — though I know it makes no sense — my own psychological and aesthetic vision.

So these pictures on my computer screen, I've begun to pretend, must be resuscitating something more than dormant memories: they feel instead as if they are — like Ida Lupino's watery eyes — striking slumbering harmonies, untethering a lineal core, because when I look at those landscapes I feel as if I'm returning to them, to a place — both physical and spiritual — where I've always been, even if I've never really been there. Looking at these pictures, I feel once again, that same "peculiar emotional intensity" that Jung describes,[8] that I've felt before when confronted by a movie that speaks to me — as if an embedded force, hibernating in some spiritual nadir, had suddenly uncoiled its limbs. Looking at these emptied landscapes, I can feel, as Jung suggested, my self dissolving into a larger collectivity.

And yet the prairies where my forebears lived — despite their hold on me — don't initially appear to be capable of harboring any esoteric, symbolic force. The Great Plains, after all, is defined by its very absence of features: it has no mountains, no hills, barely any trees, barely any rivers or lakes — just mile upon mile of grass as far as the eye can see. Every road in the Dakotas looks the same. In the images of the highway around Selby, South Dakota, where my mother's father's parents Stener and Gertrude Hilde first settled in the 1880s, the land is flat. One two-lane road stretches through fields of grass and wheat beneath a towering pasteboard sky to the edge of the horizon where one lone tree hovers like a blot of brushed ink above the fields. The land around Fairdale, North Dakota, in the northeast corner of the state, where my mother's mother's parents Henry Jeglum and Nellie Flugekvam Jeglum settled in the 1890s, looks much the same: one patch of flatness stretching off to the edge

---

8   Carl Jung, "On the Relation of Analytical Psychology to Poetry," in *The Portable Jung,* ed. Joseph Campbell, trans. R.F.C. Hull (New York: Penguin Books, 1971), 320.

of sight, with nothing but mowed grass and fields of wheat, punctuated here and there by a cylindrical bale of hay or a stand of trees planted, curiously, in one long continuous line. But even these lines of trees — the only notable feature of these landscapes — I've come to learn, are illusory: the government only planted them across the Great Plains as a means of fighting soil erosion during the Great Depression in the years after each of my grandparents had already left the farm and moved into town. But back when my grandparents were children and when their parents first settled on the Plains, there were virtually no trees as far as anyone could see in any direction.

The road that runs from Lisbon, North Dakota, near the farm where my father's mother's parents John Jorgenson and Mildred Melby Jorgenson settled around 1905, to Valley City, North Dakota, where my grandmother Alice Jorgenson Dibbern and my grandfather Hank Dibbern, my grandmother Ina Jeglum Hilde, and my step-grandfather Heinrich Hummel all went to college, consists of just one flat two-lane highway: no animals, no fences, no homes, no barns, no trees. Even the fields of wheat look indistinct — unswaying in the absence of wind, like a quilt of golden patches laid over a gentle wavering in the earth. The land around Litchville, North Dakota, where my German ancestors all lived — the Hummels, the Dibberns, the Bubachs, and the Schwandts — looks the same: an enormous rectangle of nothingness stretching off to a horizon that promises nothing but more nothingness. No fences, no animals; only an occasional one-story wooden house. Along the road from Michigan City, North Dakota, where my mother spent her first nine years, to Grand Forks, North Dakota, where she and my father first started dating and graduated from high school, two-lane highways stretch in both directions, but there's barely a car in sight. The land is flat. It seems as if the entire planet is covered with freshly-mown grass. No fences, no animals, no homes, no barns, no wheat, no trees (fig. 7).

It's not just the monotony of these landscapes, though, but the knowledge of their endless inescapability that nurtures the sensibility I soaked in as a child. The Great Plains, after all, is the

75

Fig. 7. Fairdale, ND. Screenshot from Google Street Maps.

size of Spain, France, and Germany combined. The region just rolls on and on in its pallid uniformity. My grandparents had to drive for an hour just to get to a town with even a thousand people. My grandfather Selmer Hilde, the Lutheran pastor, often had to drive eighty miles to deliver sermons at one of the rural churches that he served. But their parents and grandparents had an even more difficult time; they had to drive horse- or ox-carts for two or three days through this vacant terrain just to buy a few bags of flour to store up for the long winter.

When I was a kid and we drove through that landscape, I'd press my face up against the passenger-seat window and gaze upon those fields for hours on end. Mile after mile after mile of wheat. Then fields of soybeans and more fields of soybeans. Then fields of flax. Then fields of soybeans. Then fields of wheat. Now and then a shorn field dotted with cylindrical bales of hay. And counting those bales as they passed by my window like a motion picture was more often than not the most stimulating activity I was able to engage in over the course of the entire day. The sensation of time took on new textures; it grew dense, like the crushed-glass haze of a distant brush fire. I'd occupy myself by counting utility poles, then staring at and focusing my entire concentration on the power lines that ran between them — as if there was nothing in this world but the two-dimensionality of those lines — for as long as I could, so that my eyes would rise and fall a millimeter or two hypnotically for minutes, what seemed like dozens of minutes, as we travelled through space, tracing the gentle sloping of the power line slack from pole to pole like a Buddhist novitiate drifting off into enlightenment.

But monotony can sometimes function, surprisingly, as a wellspring. Sometimes boredom can be the seedbed of splendor. If we think of art, after all, as an object or experience that distinguishes itself from the everyday or as that which brings into focus some typically overlooked aspect of the familiar, the flatness, emptiness, and tediousness of that landscape and the remoteness and limitlessness of that sky could, paradoxically, offer up a greater potential for aesthetic epiphanies than the sublime cliff faces of Yosemite. The Great Plains' unrelenting featurelessness intensifies its most minute deviations into moments of bliss: after an hour and a half of wheat, my field of vision might instantaneously be punctuated by an astonishing outburst of sunflowers — field after field of them, with thousands upon thousands of their burnt maroon faces beaming back at me, fringed with peach, apricot, and canary yellow florets so bright I felt like my eyes or my entire being might burst into flame.

Or clouds. An entire day might pass by without seeing a single wisp in the sky — just that dull haze of a blue so pale it seemed as if the color itself was trying to inspire its own extinction. But now and then some clouds might emerge from the horizon — at first just a line or even a fleck of white — and we'd spend the entire afternoon hurtling toward them at seventy miles an hour, but almost, at any given moment, as if we weren't approaching them at all: lingering banks hugging the ground like pulled cotton dabs of Morse code communications, twenty-mile long stretches like the crevice of a canyon turned inside out or upside down. Some days the entire sky filled itself with dandelion puffs roaming through their own daydreams; other days just a miniscule flotilla of semicolons might hover on the far reaches of sight.

And then, suddenly, the clouds would be upon us — and in that moment we could see ourselves in them, no longer coming from some distant past or moving toward some unknowable future, but simply there in the present. The billows that had seemed just minutes earlier like the painted background by a third-tier Venetian artisan would loom; they'd mutate and blossom, bloom and swell, transmogrifying themselves into monumental configurations, becoming, somehow, symbolic, speaking the language of some alternative dimension yearning to expose its existence. Then in another second we'd be beneath them, and in that single instant, my neck craned back involuntarily as if by their gravitational force, I'd understand for the first time in my life, no matter how many times I'd experienced it before, that clouds were, in fact, not clouds at all, not even a thing, but mere tendrils, mere vapor, just an unfamiliar aspect of the air itself, mere hints of mist, discontinuous, not a whole thing, not an entity at all.

There is no such thing as a cloud, I would think to myself.

And then in the next second, they'd be behind me, out the back window, racing, then drifting away, then slowly solidifying so that they were, in fact, clouds, after all, but not the same ones I'd been following and falling in love with all afternoon, and I'd witness, mesmerized once again, their lingering retreat, their resistant dissipation, for all appearances utterly motionless, hour after hour, so that I came to trust in clouds once again, allowing myself once again to believe in — to pray for — the immaterial, until they became just a faint line once more above the horizon, or an off-white dapple, or a smudge, and then disappeared once more forever over the edge of the earth.

3

The Poetics of Excess ::
The Circularity of Drift

She stands alone in the middle of the living room, deploying her physicality in order to bring forth and make visible psychic states that the world is desperate to keep invisible: her creased forehead; her pinched or trembling lips; her alert eyes, scanning voraciously; her arms like compass needles; her hands and her pointing, curled, or stabbing fingers; her voice, simultaneously determined yet afraid; her torso, coiled and tensed; her free-wheeling bangs; her panting breath; and her shifting or lurching feet which are her roots into this world that she can sense is slipping. She's making of her self a register, to the extent that a register is the full range of a musical instrument. She's transforming her entire being into an emblem of resistance. She's careening forward to remind us — though we never knew it until this very moment — that it is the inscrutable periphery of experience that is the core of the human condition. She's transforming her physicality into a signal flare, a glyph of pent-up spirit, or perhaps a portal whose inadmissibility is the lure that pulls me inextricably into the scintillation of her ruin.

Her eyes are seeking, because she knows that the source of her fear is emanating from behind the door. Her eyes are reflections: cast back over her shoulder at her husband and the doctor behind the door, with just a hint of what is not quite yet a tear glistening, the visible symptom of her frenzy. She's so fixated on and so knowing about the unrelenting logic of her impending victimization that she's completely disinterested in how her hair falls down the side of her face in curled, tousled wisps, floating over her ear, drifting across her neck. She leans forward slightly on the chair, her chin cocked back toward the door. She lets her mouth hang open, slack, her lower lip not quite quivering. She hunches her shoulders and curls up her thin fingers so tightly that the knuckles of each hand are barely brushing together, as if the space between them collects the tension of her entire body, and yet she's not interested in the fact that her hands are touching, not interested that her fingers are curled up together, not interested in her body's coiled tension because she's concentrating every ounce of mental energy on the men behind the door, her gaze reflecting her fear but also — more significantly — her knowledge of that fear, fear of what she knows her husband wants to do with her but also fear of her own inability to control her body or quiet her mind, her eyes reflecting the anguish that this knowledge of her own instability will be her last remaining instrument to wield against the men who are bent on controlling her precisely because, they believe, they love her so dear.

The actress is Gena Rowlands. She's playing the character of Mabel Longhetti in the 1974 film *A Woman Under the Influence,* directed by her husband and collaborator John Cassavetes. And Rowlands — standing alone in the center of the living room of an old bungalow in working class Los Angeles — has made her character a riveting spectacle of mental collapse but also of increasingly keen perception, while she has simultaneously made her own status as an actor a riveting spectacle of a radically excessive style in contrast to the norms of classical acting that have dominated the cinema for decades.

I am 22 and I am living in San Francisco the first year after college, struggling to imagine the person I might want to become, and I'm seeing Rowlands on screen for the first time and I feel that the universe is suddenly shifting. Her performance is so arresting and so wise that I find myself conflating her and her character into a composite identity, a kaleidoscopic persona that's catalyzing my own multifaceted potential. In her deployment of herself as this philosophy of aesthetic excess, she has pulled from me a vision, a shape into which a destiny might breathe, not in my actual lived experience, but in the very habitation of thought.

The camera hovers and floats because it moves as she does. The camera's gaze is as fixated on her predicament as she is. She has made herself the center of all attention. She controls the orchestration of the image as she controls my own increasing devotion to her, to her emotional flexibility, to the way her soul seems to stagger out onto the surface of reality.

And though Mabel is cowering in the throes of a mental breakdown — or perhaps precisely because she's the one person who's suffering most egregiously — she's also the one human being in this film with the keenest sense of humanity and thus the one character possessing the greatest potential for enlightenment. Mabel, therefore, begins to defy these two men. But because the character of her husband Nick Longhetti, played by Peter Falk, is the obvious alter ego to Rowlands's real-life husband Cassavetes, the film's director — its purported solo auteur — Rowlands as an actress is simultaneously defying the cinephilic assumptions about authorship, staking her own artistic ground in the history of the art form. So the force of her will is disturbing my conception of cinema and of my own place in the world: only this whirlwind of excess — both Mabel's range of expression and Rowlands's baroque aesthetic vision — I am beginning to want to believe, can enable us to accurately perceive the world around us and thus to plant our roots firmly in its soil.

In the scene unfolding before me, descending into the bleak heart of the story, Rowlands is taking the art of film itself along with her into an intensive examination of the minutiae of the moment, ultimately laying bare the fundamentally extravagant dimension of the quotidian. And sitting alone in that darkened theater, in my then-youthful openness, Rowlands is becoming

Fig. 8. Screenshot from *A Woman under the Influence* (dir. John Cassavetes, 1974).

my new icon, my beacon, because she is the polar opposite of the idea of austerity that I've accepted as my cultural inheritance. She is the countervailing Jungian force that yearns to liberate me from my past and from myself. And because she is the paramount vehicle of cinematic excess, the avatar of art's revelatory power, she will become, I am beginning to understand, the North Star of my new sensibility.

The deeper Mabel descends into her mania, the more emphatically Rowlands begins to assert her own authority as the force that will shape this film: she stands, then moves across the room as Nick leads the doctor in from the front door. Mabel knows and we know suddenly why he's here. And we see her mind working, calculating her routes of escape from the inevitable. The camera captures her body from head to toe in the frame for the first time, and it is only by seeing her entire body that we begin to understand her: Rowlands deploys the furthest extent of her physicality and the entire breadth of the frame to express the inexpressible nuances of Mabel's intensity and fragility, which are our own. Her pink socks and her tousled hair and her thigh-length embroidered hippie dress are the visible signature of her force in the world, of her own strategic performance of life at its most vibrant, of her joy and her hope, of her defiance in the face of a world gone grim, while they are, at the same time, the visible signature of her insecure foothold in this world, of her unremitting unravelling, and of her slippage.

The sequence, too, unravels — so painfully slowly that it challenges our expectations of time, emphasizing its pliability, so that the seconds and minutes begin to take on unexpected sensual qualities, pulsing and heaving, almost buckling in on themselves, the filmmaking a spectacle of its own hyper-aes-theticization, its inordinate style the uneasy analogue of Mabel's own mental dissolution.

Rowlands keeps pushing stylistic excess as far as it can go because Mabel's psychic collapse this time, we come to see, is worse than ever before. This may be because earlier that after-noon, her husband Nick — who's painfully in love with her but painfully ill-equipped to deal with this breakdown — slapped her in the face, slapped her for what we suspect might have been the first time, and now is stalking, circling her, threatening to have her committed, standing between her and his mother, who commands the stairwell like a witch with her sweep of gray hair and her wicked blue eye shadow, guarding the only route to the children safely in bed upstairs, while the doctor roams the room behind Mabel with his black bag, which, Mabel knows, keeps the syringe that will put her to sleep, the agent of her impending institutionalization.

And Mabel's psychic extravagance creates its own magnetic field, pulling every other character into its orbit, turning the entire scene into a solar system of unleashed repressions. The mother-in-law comes down the stairs and the camera follows her as she bellows and cackles, yelling to the doctor that this woman has to go, that she's crazy, that her son tells her things, that she lets the kids run around naked and hungry, and Mabel in the background begins to blur, the image of her personhood unfocusing, as the hand-held camera follows the mother-in-law who's shouting and pointing — held back by the doctor, then held back by her son — trying to elude their grasp, surging for-ward like a wave of scalding fingernails to claw at Mabel's body.

But it's only then, when the scene reaches what must be the climax because things can't possibly get any worse, that the film begins to sway and surge, and I am swaying and surging in cadence with the film and with Rowlands's increasingly iconoclastic performance, as the seams of this family and of the entire movie — and perhaps, even, the seams of the cinema itself — begin to rip apart. Because then, as Rowlands takes her character even deeper into oblivion, drifting, inarticulate, wobbling on her feet as she tries to speak, raising her arms as if warding off cobwebs descending from an unseen mist, blinking from a piercing beam whose mysterious source only she can penetrate, her eyes lolling upward, Nick sees the doctor preparing his syringe and suddenly makes a decision. He grabs her body close to his chest the way he must have done hundreds of times before in the darkened, late-night stillness of their bedroom and yells that he loves her, that he loves her, and the movie in that instant performs an about-face on itself, so that as the doctor approaches, holding the needle aloft, the madness and excess of this scene, we suddenly realize, hasn't even begun, because at this moment, Peter Falk as an actor takes the movie with him into a whole other dimension, entering into the bubble of Rowlands's actorly delirium with her, turning on the doctor and screaming at him to get away, then turning back to his wife and telling her again that he loves her, and she falls back limply in his arms, her gaze drifting to the ceiling.

But then Rowlands exerts her hold on the film once again: as the doctor tells her he'd like to give her a sedative to calm her down, Mabel comes to her senses and pushes back. She leaps forward at him, indignant and enraged, making a cross with her fingers as if she's warding off Satan himself, hissing at him to get back in his coffin. But with that gesture she realizes that she's finally taken it one step too far, that everyone now is finally against her, that there's no hope anymore if there ever had been, that everything's closing in on her and she falls back into the living room to make her last stand, starting to bargain with them. "Don't take me to the hospital, just let me stay in the house. I don't need to go away." Then she's pointing a manic accusing finger at the doctor because she knows that she is the only one who can really see, and screams, "You're the one who's sick! You're the one who needs a doctor!"[1]

And in that darkened theater I know now that I have completely fallen under the spell of Rowlands's stylistic indulgence because at that very moment of revelation, she takes the movie yet again even further into its own emotional wreckage as Mabel suddenly remembers the children, and her face lights up, and just when I'd begun to hope that maybe now the scene must finally be coming to an end, that finally now we'd get our reprieve, yet again all hell breaks loose even worse than ever before and I find myself swaying and surging in cadence with both Rowlands and the film once again as Mabel rushes up the stairs to save the children, the only sane person in the house who actually remembers the children, the only sane person in the entire world, the only one who cares about the children, the only one who loves them, then suddenly everyone is upstairs in the children's room, the mother-in-law, the doctor, and all three children grabbing onto Mabel like one giant rugby scrum, holding her down on a child's bed as she tries to get loose from the mother-in-law and the doctor's control as the kids are grabbing at Mabel trying to get her free and Nick comes into the room and everyone's yelling and crying and screaming and Mabel is calling out to her husband to help her and then she manages to break free and grab her son away from them and Nick grabs him back away from her, and then the scene cuts suddenly and finally it's all over.

And yet this is not how I remember the movie. It couldn't possibly be — to see and to hear the film and to remember it so vividly. No. I can only see it this way, more than twenty-five years after that first experience, after watching and re-watching and re-watching that sequence. No. The only thing I can really remember from that first screening is a feeling.

---

1   John Cassavetes, dir., *A Woman Under the Influence* (1974; Criterion Collection, 2013), Blu-Ray disc, 1:10:29–1:23:44.

I remember Gena Rowlands. I remember her face, the way she clenched her forehead into one long crease. I remember the way she raised her eyebrows into a perilous arch. I remember her wide-eyed, fixed, unblinking gaze. I remember the way she held her arms akimbo like a scarecrow in a field of flame. I remember the way she blew her bangs from her eyes out of the corner of her mouth and the way she pointed with her thumbs like a drunken sailor trying to hitch a ride. I remember the camera hovering, tracing her disoriented peregrinations across the living room floor. I remember the feeling of being subjugated to the relentlessness of time. I remember time's ceaseless unwinding. I remember the spiraling into desolation. I remember it was as if I'd discovered a doorway into a hidden dimension. And I remember my gut. The empty hollow of my stomach. My body quivering. I remember almost panting at this slow-motion unspooling catastrophe which was also my exhilaration.

I'd fallen for her because the states of consciousness — or the modes of existence — that she was exploring and expressing were antithetical to the ideas of restraint and reserve that I'd come to believe I'd been raised with. Her exorbitant withering was an antidote against my legacy — both the aridity of the desert and the emptiness of the Great Plains — that might release and thus normalize my repressed extravagance.

But in Rowlands's and Cassavetes's world, a woman on the cusp of oblivion doesn't represent an anomalous or peripheral state. Her inability to forge meaningful human connections, her despair and ruin, are instead central, fundamental states of the human condition, and it is the others who surround her — men who are able to function within society's unwritten rules — who are, in fact, the ones who are actually living on the periphery, pale reflections of this female protagonist, estranged from human consciousness's home. Mabel's ostensible mental cataclysm is, then, the product of her acute perceptions and her eagerness to inhabit the fullness of her desires, while Rowlands's overwrought expressivity represents an astute challenge to the repressed standards of aesthetic history. So by surrendering to Rowlands and her artistic excess that day in that movie theater,

I was connecting with the quintessence of human character and ultimately, beginning to cultivate the full range of my own.

§

I was living in San Francisco, in the Height-Ashbury with a then-boyfriend, the first year after college, just 22-years-old. I didn't have the slightest idea then what I was going to do with my life. I couldn't imagine a career. I couldn't imagine a way to make money that could ever possibly make me happy. Instead, I worked a series of dead-end temp jobs nine to five to make ends meet. I did data entry, filed papers in rows of six-foot-tall filing cabinets, assembled color-coded batches of manila folders-within-manila folders for weeks on end, or just sat alone in a cubicle staring off into space, pretending to be busy all day long. In retrospect, I was a naïve kid; I didn't really know much of anything. None of us did. How could we? I'd never had to be an adult before. And in San Francisco in those pre-Internet days, with its dirty streets, bad transit, rampant unemployment, and homelessness, it was easy to feel unmoored.

The only thing I really cared about back then was language. When I wasn't at work, I was inhaling poetry, as you only can when you're young and every single book you come across is a discovery. I'd already begun to develop, I thought then, aesthetic tastes and thus a worldview more sophisticated than I'd had just a year before. I was distancing myself, at first hesitantly, then wholeheartedly, from my earlier attachment to the plain-spoken poets of the American Midwest I'd admired in college. More and more I was finding myself drawn to poets inspired by transcendent and metaphysical impulses, poets who found their lineage not in the language of the common people but in the irrationality of dreams, poets who explored language's exclusive access — its direct channel — to the heightened states of euphoria and bliss, but also to the quagmires of bewilderment and dread. I was young and impressionable. I was seeking something other than what I was. I was rejecting reticence and restraint. I was searching, instead, for the aesthetic analogues of magma and geysers, caverns and constellations, forest fires and flooding rivers. And in my off hours, late at night or on weekends or during the weeks when I was unemployed, I was trying to write poetry — or perhaps more accurately, trying to become the type of person who was a poet.

When I first saw Gena Rowlands, I understood immediately that she was pointing the way. She reminded me of the poets that I'd begun falling for — like César Vallejo, Paul Celan, and Hart Crane — poets who were extending the possibilities of language so that they seemed no longer to be writing in Spanish, German, or English but were inventing instead some new modes of expression that maintained only a tangential relationship to their native tongue, language that, like Rowlands's hyperkinesis and verbal tics, was trying to pierce through the scrim of existence by drawing on esoteric sources of illumination. "So, dead immortal," Vallejo had written. "Between the colonnade of your bones which cannot fall even in weeping, and in whose side even Destiny cannot slide one of his fingers. So dead immortal. So."[2] I read those sentences sitting up in bed late at night, trying to understand how one could be both dead and immortal — though I knew instinctively that we all were — trying to picture the colonnade of my own bones within my own body, though I knew it was impossible to understand what that might even mean, which was exactly why I'd fallen in love with it. Or Celan, who wrote that the "journey-sickles at the extraheavenly place mime themselves white-gray into moon-swallows together, into star swifts."[3] And I grappled, sitting up in bed late at night, with the notion of a journey that was also a sickle or a sickle that was also a journey, of how this journey — or of how any noun — might, in fact, mime itself into anything, much less a star swift, whatever that might be, though I knew also that the very reason I loved the star swift was because I'd

2   César Vallejo, "Trilce XLV," trans. Charles Tomlinson and Henry Gifford, *Poetry* 109, no. 4 (1967): 232–33.

3   Author's translation, from Paul Celan, *Poems of Paul Celan: Revised and Expanded,* trans. Michael Hamburger (New York: Persea Books, 2002), 260.

never be able to articulate a coherent definition, though I also somehow knew — or at least I thought that maybe I knew — precisely what it was. Or Crane. My idol. My beloved. "Take this sea," Crane wrote, "whose diapason knells, on scrolls of silver snowy sentences, the sceptered terror of whose sessions rends, as her demeanors motion well or ill, all but the pieties of lovers' hands."[4] And I read that sentence, sitting up in bed late at night, over and over again. And again. And again. I traced my finger over the sentences on the surface of the page, in effervescent bewilderment, loving it precisely because I could not comprehend.

Witnessing those heightened states — even from a place of confusion — felt liberating and epiphanic. But exalted language like that also had the opposite effect in that it repeatedly foregrounded the incessant tedium of the everyday, and thus of the burning necessity of escape. And everyday life in San Francisco back then was unremittingly pressing its inadequacy into me. Monday morning to Friday morning, I'd take the 7 bus or the 71 or the N train downtown to a dead-end temp job in an ugly office tower where I'd sit in a cubicle all day typing useless information into a database or filling out a stack of forms or standing in front of the Xerox machine making copies for hours on end or just shifting stacks of forms around on my desk pretending to be busy. Then in my off hours at night or on weekends or during the weeks when I was unemployed, I kept writing poetry.

But when I put pen to paper I never quite managed to achieve those same levels of elevated consciousness as Vallejo, Celan, and Crane had been able to reach. My surrealism was nonsensical, not resonant. I was incapable, it seemed, of expressing the inexpressible.

I kept writing, though. Night after night after night, on weekends and throughout the long weeks when I was unemployed, sitting in coffee houses or sitting up in bed late at night. And I

---

4   Hart Crane, "Voyages," in *The Complete Poems of Hart Crane,* ed. Marc Simon (New York: Liveright, 2000), 35.

kept mailing my poems off to small literary magazines. And I kept receiving rejections: rejection after rejection after rejection.

But those were also the years I felt myself shifting. Where once I'd stay up late parsing the words of Celan with dictionary at hand, more and more I found my mind drifting, circling back over the movies I'd begun seeing obsessively at the city's revival houses: taking the 7 or the 71 or the 33 bus or the N-line or the BART or even a cable car to or from the Red Vic or the Roxy or the San Francisco Art Institute or the Castro Theater or the Pacific Film Archive over in Berkeley, where I fell into a two-week-long haze when I was finally able to see the Andy Warhol films I'd fantasized about in my last years at college.

Warhol quickly joined Rowlands in my pantheon of cinematic excess, another possible icon of identification for me. I was drawn to them both because they'd each invented an aesthetic zone to inhabit beyond the boundaries of acceptable conventions. Warhol's impishly cavalier queerness was another draw. At the time, after all, the most obvious option for crafting an identity different from the one I'd inherited was to embrace my gayness. But ideas about gay identity at the time, seemingly so radical on the surface, so often fell into a genre-bound narrative arc: the confusing, painful, closeted adolescence, the melodramatic scene of coming out, and the eventual adult acceptance of one's self. Each of these moments did, in fact, ring true for me — powerfully so, in fact. But the notion of acceptance, as healthy as it was in real life, pointed to attitudes about normalcy that I instinctively wanted to escape. The nonconformist singularity I was able to come into contact with occasionally at the movies seemed much more fertile grounds for intellectual self-invention.

And Warhol, like Rowlands, was the perfect vehicle. His movies were outlandish in every possible way, eccentric like no other iconoclastic artist. I found myself sinking into them: the exhilarating boredom of *Eat,* where the artist Robert Indiana in an eerily tight and gauzy close-up nibbles on a mushroom for the entirety of a 30-minute film reel; the alienating delight of *Pretty Little Rich Girl,* starring Edie Sedgwick, an extravagantly vacuous oddity in which Sedgwick pushes acting to its limits by doing virtually nothing for thirty minutes, lounging on a bed, half-dressed, bored, indulging in her own prettiness, listening to records, smoking cigarettes, applying lipstick, making inane, barely audible small talk with a figure offscreen, a movie whose intransigent apathy Warhol exacerbates by leaving one of the two reels intentionally out of focus; the claustrophobic two-reel nightmare of *The Life of Juanita Castro* and the claustrophobic two-reel nightmare of *Vinyl*; the ultra-rare feature *Bike Boy* that opens with a hauntingly long take of a dumb hunk soaping himself up in the shower, staring mute and hollow-eyed and uncomfortable into offscreen space waiting for directions that never come; the split-screen projection of *Chelsea Girls,* made up of fourteen thirty-minute reels of unbelievable torpor projected side-by-side — Nico cutting her bangs in a kitchen, making mumbled small talk with a friend as the camera makes unmotivated pans and zooms, a balding old queen in a bath towel and two female friends listlessly undressing a handsome younger man, Brigid Polk bitching to a friend about her drug habit, a foursome of mean-spirited drug-addled women lounging on a bed, the camera panning and zooming irrationally, sound going in and out irrationally, the image going in and out of focus irrationally, drag queens and butch trade, inexhaustibly boring and stupidly intense close-ups of Factory hangers-on in psychedelic searchlight washes of blue and red, Eric Emerson, dazed by drugs, undressing and lazily caressing his torso, showing off his arms and chest, his hairy stomach, his ass, his pubic hair, teasing us with the outline of his cock in his blue jeans, a bevy of silent figures in Caravaggio-esque strobing profiles, then Nico again, in an intensely bright color close-up for thirty minutes, while Ondine in his most flagrantly bitchy and haggard performance in black and white on the right side of the screen shoots up, then goes on a rant for an entire reel, a nonsensical, boring, interminable, painfully stupid rant, the emotional climax of the film, better than anyone else able to personify Warhol's discomforting fascination with the nastiness born of lethargy, slapping and punching a woman who comes in to talk to him,

91

calling her a lousy creep, a miserable phony, a dumb bitch, while all along in the opposite screen to the left, Warhol treats Nico's face as a reverential canvas, throwing colored polka-dots and bright white slashes across her beautiful, soulless face. My two-week-long Warhol obsession culminated with the most intriguingly enigmatic of his pictures, *Lonesome Cowboys,* shot over the course of five days on the lot of a tourist attraction Old West town on the outskirts of Tucson, Arizona, where a handful of drug-addled gay men from Manhattan ad-libbed ad nauseam, acting out what they imagined to be the essential nature of masculine heterosexuality, which thus ended up as a nasty little story about their sexual subjugation of Warhol's frequent collaborator, the superstar Viva, a movie that was so compelling because it seemed simultaneously totally ignorant and yet self-reflexively critical of its own cruelty. Warhol's ostentatious disinterest in the dominant conventions of filmmaking, his ostentatious refusal to articulate any moral judgments, his ostentatious disregard for the standards of representing gay sexuality at the time, became, like Rowlands's inappropriate histrionics, a paradigm for me. His aesthetic strangeness lured me in, inspiring me to keep going deeper into the movies. And I did, every other night back to the Castro Theater — the old movie palace, my temple, with its vaulted ceilings and chandelier, its balcony, its murals on the walls, its organ that rose from beneath the stage — where I saw Douglas Sirk's Brechtian Hollywood Fifties melodramas for the first time, Pier Paolo Pasolini's *Salo,* and week upon week of B-noirs that were tawdrily similar and tawdrily forgettable.

But all this time, my mind kept circling back to the image of Gena Rowlands. She became a fixture for me. Her haunted gestures and her vatic kinetics had lured me in; I was intrigued by how she'd transformed her physicality into a kind of philosophy, an exploration of the inherent extravagance of futility. On the bus in the morning on my way to work, on the bus in the evening on my way home, sitting up in bed at home on a weeknight with a pen in hand and a notebook on my lap trying to write, or in a coffee shop on my days off with a pen in hand and a notepad on the table trying to write, she began to seep into me.

And inexorably — as if mesmerized by the orbits of the outer planets — I found myself writing about her: long, meandering fragments, scribbled notes and aimless descriptions, scraps of images that began to take nascent cinematic shape.

I saw Rowlands leaning against a concrete alley wall, glancing over her shoulder as if twisting in a modernist ballet, afraid of something or someone looming in off-screen space. I saw her thumbing a ride on the outskirts of a town in the desert, shabby chartreuse suitcase at her feet, a cigarette dangling from her lips. I saw her roving through landscapes, the flat desert scrub brush of the Arizona-California border, the rolling sage and olive hills of northwestern New Mexico covered by twisting mimosa trees, the same landscapes we used to drive through summer after summer when I was young on the way to visit grandparents in North Dakota and Minnesota. I imagined Rowlands escaping from tedium, in the middle of a journey, drifting through a disjointed elongation of time.

I wrote draft after draft of poems about Rowlands, poems that began to unfold — without conscious intent — as long, dissonant collages of images and scenes, messy assemblages of phrases splayed across the page, imaginary films with Rowlands at their core. I was writing about her, but I was channeling myself. And as these fitful phantasms began to take shape in partial sentences separated by vast white chasms across the page, she sometimes took on a more concrete role as a character, if only fleetingly: as a retired former diplomat living on the edge of Taos, struggling to connect with her estranged daughter; as a chain-smoking waitress standing outside a cheap café in Durango; as a journalist visiting an archeological dig, stepping gingerly across wooden planks laid down across a vast, semicircular, chalky orange pit. But the more I wrote, the more these narratives failed to congeal. Or, perhaps, the more I began to resist. Something slumbering within fought back against any attempt to contain her. I was losing interest in making meaning out of her fluidity. She lived more actively in my imagination as an inconstant notion, a candle flame, the roving eye of a hurricane.

Over the years, this daydreaming took over and the poetry slowly fell away. I came to inhabit my fragmentary imaginings more than I did my forever-unrealized texts. Rowlands choreographed her nettlesome energy throughout the stages of my mental drift, surrounding herself with vast ellipses of her own disappearances in order to save me from settling into a premature coherence. And the fragments just kept unspooling, so much so that I began to have suspicions: the daydreaming, it seemed to me, felt more creative than the writing. Writing, after all, requires us to force our ideas into specific language; it directs us to make the imagination concrete, but by doing so, it ultimately brings our dreaming to an end. A poem is an opening, but also a closing of the mind. A written document is a kind of death.

Daydreaming, on the other hand, is boundless. In the unfinished — and thus unfettered — imagination, I could dwell in that very excess that had attracted me to Rowlands, and to the movies, in the first place. The image of Sedgwick out of focus, splaying her barely-clothed erotic torso diagonally across a bed, Nico's glacial visage dappled by flashing psychedelic dots challenging the camera's gaze, crooked rain-drenched film noir streets bathed in midnight neon, steam rooms of chiaroscuro opulence, back alleys and boxing gyms, dingy bars and fleabag hotels, all flickered through me to form one long consonant stream of memory, one synthetic cacophony of the interior. Mental life was all sparks and shadows, imagistic slivers and forgettings, the inconsistent thrum brought on by the movies. In daydreams, it came to seem, I could achieve that state of liberating emotional profusion I aimed for, contrary to the monochromatic asceticism I'd imagined as my birthright.

Rowlands's image came to me in landscapes — always the American Southwest, because, I'd begun to suspect, the desert's barren majesty made my ingrained affinity for moderation and isolation seem consequential; it spoke to me of home and thus of our innate need to transform home. She came to me in widescreen shots of flat expanses dotted with scrub brush and palo verde trees, mountain ranges so distant they appeared like a powdered haze. I saw her standing against an ochre cliff face, an incongruous figure in her blue paisley dress and oversized sunglasses. I saw her surrounded by ocotillo bushes — their long, spindly arms of spiky needles waving gently like ghostly flickers of olive-green flame in the foreground of the purple night. I saw her straying from her intentions, lost in a circle of towering lime-blue agave. I saw her dwarfed by monumental lavender boulders. I saw her climbing over orange promontories to gaze out over valleys of tan, sandy dirt and scrawny pale bushes that looked like parched death. I imagined her in landscapes because their grandeur highlighted humanity's insignificance. Emphasizing her personhood by means of the land was one of my unconscious mind's mechanisms for eradicating our traditional notions of character — and thus of identity itself.

The vastness of these landscapes immobilized her, but — almost as if from a need to counteract the land and the sky's dominion over us — I often imagined her in motion. I saw her exhausted, half-asleep in the back of a bus with her head leaning against smudged glass, gazing distractedly now and then out the window, now and then brushing a loose strand of hair from her forehead, disinterested in the earth's incessant expansion beyond the limits of vision. I saw her rambling along a path into a copse of twisted mesquite trees. I saw her walking in circles in a claustrophobic backyard surrounded by brick walls. I saw her sneaking through an alley. I saw her hitching rides. I saw her dozing off in the cab of a semi. I saw her in the back of a pickup on a lone desert highway. I saw her at the wheel, driving toward a bleak horizon outside Fresno or Bakersfield, furrowed fields like charred wax creeping to the top of the frame.

But her origin and her destination always remained obscure. I could never picture her at either the beginning or the end. She could not embody those points on any line. She was, instead, suspended in the exploration of some interstitial zone. She was the kernel of an unformed idea, a mere splinter of time. But travel without a destination is not travel at all: it is a condition. And this transitory state of consciousness, this refusal to transgress boundaries, this fundamental thirst to flourish in the core of the infinite threshold, was the very opposite, ironically, of the heightened states I'd come to associate with Rowlands and the poetry of excess that I loved. Her motionless motion, her quiescence in this circular vagabonding, was the product of my own dilapidated imagination. Her resolute and indefatigable futurelessness was my vision. Like me, she was only half-leaving the past: I could not picture her destination because I could not picture my own.

I wrote drafts and drafts of poems about Rowlands — desultory, purgative sprawls — but I could never finish a single one. They unspooled, without structure, without any conception of an ending, and the more I wrote the more structureless they became. Their drift was the aesthetics of hopelessness. And yet, their disorder was also a challenge to the conventions of narrative, which exist to feed our illusion that we can make coherent meaning of our lives. And my gradual submission to such untethered imaginings was drawing me simultaneously closer to the movies, since movies were — with their imagistic iconicity and their spatial and temporal discontinuity — daydreams made glorious. I was slowly seeping into a lifestyle of intensive cinephilia, which was, I was slowly beginning to convince myself, not merely a passive activity, but, in fact, one of the single most efficient catalysts of the creative life. So I decided to give up. I moved from San Francisco to New York. I put my books of Vallejo, Celan, and Crane up on the shelf where they remain to this day. I gave up on writing poetry. I went to the movies instead.

I could picture Rowlands back in those days only in those caesuras because her immobility was the product of the irreconcilability of origin and destination. Identity is not a fixed point. It is, instead, a continual reiteration of the insuperable conflicts between the past and the future that our culture has bestowed upon us. Identity is not a path, but a kind of suspension, an immaterial floating within a portal that we can never entirely traverse. We cannot cross boundaries. We cannot even see the perimeter. Futility is our essence. We are the lacuna in the center of the centerless atmosphere.

But this suspended animation breeds paradox. Because if the inherited traits that undergird our unconscious invent their own systems to counteract themselves, every dream breeds its own antithesis. The dream of escape to an idealized future is always, inevitably, a dream about the return to origins, but to origins we will never be able to locate since origins are always an arbitrary fiction we've invented to make sense of ourselves. The future is always a returning to the past. Identity is circular. There is no journey. There is only stasis. And the illusion of hope. Rowlands's liminal state was my mind's churning through this impossibility.

These days, if I will my memories of Rowlands from my youth back up to the surface, I see her standing at the mouth of a canyon. Her face is now a placid mask. She glances behind her at the hills rolling off into dissolution. She glances before her at the sinuous passage between sheer cliffs. We can imagine what lies beyond: wolves and deer, hawks and eagles, waterfalls and soundless glades, all nourished by a river of sapphire blue thundering its way to an alluvial plain. The canyon walls are prismatic because they are the phantasm of a future.

Now I see Gena Rowlands turning her face to me. Now I see her occupying abstract space. Now I know that time is falling away, spiraling in on itself, that time is never present, that time is always and only a continual plummeting away. Rowlands looks down at an object in the palm of her hand. In a close-up, we see through her eyes. It is a family photograph, black and white, creased and faded, decades old. In a room so unadorned it functions as pure metaphor, an old woman stands behind a chair where a young mother sits, holding a baby. The grandmother's wrinkled face beams. The mother's porcelain demeanor pierces us. The baby's angelic face is a howling blur. But this is no actual photograph. It exists only as I've imagined it. These three figures are the circle of eternity: my grandmother, my mother, and me.

4

Images of Others ::
Images of Ourselves

If the yearning for the future is always a circling back to the past, always the need, once again, to revive history in order to both inhabit and to eviscerate it, it's no surprise that I find myself returning now and then to peruse those grainy, faded, and creased black-and-white images I've managed to recover from the old family photo albums.

In truth, though, there are only a few family photographs I've come across that keep resonating with me today. There's one photograph, in particular, I keep returning to — perhaps, not surprisingly, because it's the one picture I've found that's most unlike the other images I've collected. I'm drawn to it because it's the most uncharacteristically artistic photograph — and thus the most uncharacteristically uncanny image of all the old family pictures. I've fallen for it because it evokes a sense of my family's past that seems alluringly unfamiliar to me.

In this favorite image, my great-grandmother Gertrude Johnson Hilde, a white-haired, plump, almost eighty-year-old woman in a plain cotton dress stands in a vast expanse of faded colorlessness, a sweeping field of grass and an empty haze of sky that bisects the frame, her back to the camera, one arm outstretched, pointing, searching into offscreen space: for what, it's not immediately clear (fig. 9). She is standing, my mother explains to me as we examine the photograph together almost seventy years after the fact, on the land of the farm where she, her husband Stener, and their first five children once lived, back before my grandfather Selmer was born. But the farm, obviously, is no longer there at the time when this photograph was taken in 1951. She is searching, my mother explains to me, for the grave of her daughter Alma, who died as an infant in 1898. Alma's grave is somewhere nearby, but my great-grandmother clearly can't remember where, exactly. She is pointing off into the distance, at something indistinct even to her, a memory which has transformed itself over the decades into a spatial confusion. She's explaining to her son — my grandfather's brother Andrew, my mother suspects — that before he was born, more than fifty years before this photo was taken, her entire life and those of her husband and children flourished in this space that has now become an enigma. She is, like me, trying to return to her past as a way of understanding her present and as a way of shaping the future for her children and her descendants. But her attempt, like my own, is fundamentally futile because the past is no longer visible to her; the past has become an illusion. She is pointing, it seems, at nothing. At nothingness itself. At an absence. At the space memory wants to fill, which is both the epicenter and the boundary line of all our attachments and all our aversions.

The photograph moves me because her gesture toward the core of emptiness highlights the image's unlikely mystery and artistry. It moves me also, I suspect, because this family member feels like a stranger to me. I never met my great-grandmother Gertrude Hilde. I don't remember ever hearing a single story about her. She doesn't look like me or like anyone else in the family. My mother herself met her only once, she thinks, before she died when my mother was just a girl. She is the mother of my mother's father, whom I knew well, but I don't remember him telling me any stories about her. She is, to me, a conundrum. So I return to an image like this, ironically, not because

Fig. 9. Gertrude Johnson Hilde. Courtesy of the author

it's representative but precisely because it's atypical — in both style and substance — as if its difference reveals some concealed truths ingrained in my imagined background, some alternative history of my origins and thus some alternative characteristics hibernating within, but still imperceptible to me.

Of all the images I've found from the old family albums, this is the oldest one that might be called a snapshot, the earliest image I've found that wasn't staged, and it's the picture's improvisatory flair that gives it the air of art, distinguishing it from a mere historical document. The chance encounter with the camera has turned my great-grandmother — the farmer's wife from Alberta, Canada — into an aesthetic vehicle of modernist disquiet. Her bemusement is palpable, as if she is simultaneously absorbing from and radiating into the surrounding atmosphere all the apprehensions of a newly irreligious age. Unable to see what she wants to see, she's vibrating with the intensity of her unfulfilled need. My great-grandmother's soul bursts out from her body; her aura is aflame.

And the aleatory nature of the snapshot has turned this photographer into an artist as well, enabling him to capture the ineffable. This image feels cinematic. It emblematizes the allure of doubt, a secular vision of modernity. So I have to remind myself every time I return to it that the man who took this picture — the auteur of this visual panegyric to the magnificence of uncertainty — must have been my grandfather Selmer, the Lutheran pastor himself, the one person in my family's history whom I'd most associate, ironically, with the certainty of religious belief.

My grandmother Ina is no longer here to tell me what this image means, but the caption from the old family photo album tells me that this is the Missouri Bluffs outside Selby, South Dakota, where the Hilde farmstead — "Stener's buildings," it says — once stood. The caption, though, tells me virtually nothing about the photograph's larger meaning. I've only been able to understand its story by talking to my mother and by uncovering old family documents.

The picture depicts my great-grandmother Gertrude Hilde in 1951 on a trip from her home on a farm in Alberta — where my grandfather Selmer was born in 1907 — back to the land outside Selby, South Dakota, where she and her husband had farmed between 1881 and 1902. It was the first time she'd returned in 49 years. She'd come back at the invitation of my grandfather, then living in the town of Michigan City, North Dakota, in order to find the grave of her daughter Alma, the only one of her twelve children who'd died in infancy. She was returning to her own past as I am returning to my own whenever I look at her. Hers is the great circling, the quest for knowledge we know that we will never know, like the knowledge of God, the rejection of which I've considered for more than three decades now, perhaps falsely, as a fundamental aspect of my personality, an act that distinguished me from the ancestors who still, nevertheless, cast their spell over me.

In a letter he wrote to his mother, inviting her down to the old farmstead, Selmer described his quest to find Alma's gravestone in a visit he'd made one year earlier. In the language of a man educated in Lutheran theology, but also clearly the language of a son trying to assuage his mother's lingering pain, he writes how impossible it was to find the grave because all the old farm buildings had long since been torn down, because history had been erased in that part of the plains. "Finally," he wrote, we came to the cemetery from the south. My heart was deeply stirred as I thought of the day when little Alma Paulene was laid to rest and the grief of those who mourned. If only we would be able to find her last resting place. It would be good for the soul to find it. At least we could know that she had arrived home safely even though we could not be so sure of some of the rest of us.

And then, suddenly, the local farmer's wife who was serving as his guide found Alma's headstone and cried out, "Here it is." "And was I ever thrilled," wrote Selmer:

It was rather hard to have to leave the cemetery. It was holy ground to me. And the earnest prayer ascended to heaven that we all might be permitted to be united in heaven — that when that day dawns, none of us would be missing.

Why do we believe that Alma now is there? Because of what God has promised in His Word. Rejecting His Word we have no authority for faith and life and therefore live without hope. But in His Word God has promised to receive us in baptism. In holy baptism Alma became a child of God. There was nothing she could do as a helpless infant to win acceptance by God. Nor her parents. It was God who in His infinite wisdom and love received her by grace. And so we too must be saved. Not by our works of righteousness but by faith in the righteous works of God who sent His only begotten Son to be our Savior. It is faith in Christ that saves. Faith accepts Him.

The theology that undergirds my grandfather's language seems alien to me now and to most of the contemporary world. I haven't gone to church, after all, since I was in my teens. Instead of church, I visit its secular equivalents: museums and concert halls and revival house movie theaters, the nonreligious homes of my obsessive acts of devotion. Yet my grandfather's words are not that strange, after all; they do not ring hollow. They resonate with me because I, too, was raised in the Lutheran church and the Lutheran church's language is my own. From my earliest years, I've heard pastors utter words so similar, the theology has sunk deep into my mind's oldest sediments. The vision of eternal life bound in faith alone — justification exclusively through God's grace rather than through good deeds — echoes back five hundred years to the teachings of Martin Luther himself.

And yet, a countercurrent to this redemptive power of belief runs through the Protestant vision as well — though pastors rarely acknowledge it. More than other religions, Christianity makes belief central to salvation. And this binary and reductive conception of redemption has, admittedly, a powerfully positive allure: all you need to do is have faith, accept Jesus, and you will be granted eternal life. It's all so beautifully simple. And yet this positive force has a logically intertwined negative companion. God's absence and His unrelenting silence make belief fundamentally non-rational. Doubt, instead, seems the more obviously logical position to take. Christian philosophy, then, is dependent upon — though typically only implicitly — the act of entertaining doubt, confusion, and skepticism because God's silence inevitably makes the questioning of faith the intrinsic source of faith itself. Faith, we might say, can only exist in tandem with — and as the product of — its agnostic twin.

The centrality of doubt, though, can never be voiced aloud in church. Like the unconscious conflicts that drive our personalities, doubt needs to find release to make faith valid and to make us whole. But since it cannot make its presence known in the religious sphere, it must therefore mask itself in an unfamiliar guise, finding it easier to surface in the church's secular parallel. This is why so much ostensibly secular abstract art in the Western tradition — Kazimir Malevich's black square, Wassily Kandinsky's *Compositions,* Mark Rothko's saturated oranges and reds — are so obviously paeans to God. Art is the staging ground for the enigmas that religion cannot allow itself to explore. God's silence gives birth to art's celebration of indeterminacy, which is the obverse partner of faith, and this is why art's inherent mystery is, ultimately, as equally redemptive as — and intimately linked with — the certainty we ascribe to universal truths.

Thus, I use this photograph of my great-grandmother as the secular version of a religious icon, which is, perhaps, art's fundamental function. Pointing off at a vast gray nothingness, she draws me in like a character from some obscure art film from the 1960s; the image's unsettling expanse reminds me of Michelangelo Antonioni's investigations of modernity's emotional decay. Its implacably horizontal and pallid landscape is, like Antonioni's rocky, barren islands amid the Tyrrhenian Sea in *L'Avventura,* the visible sign of the spiritual aridity that undergirds the contemporary world. My great-grandmother is searching for meaning from the inside of a psychic chasm, and this image of a small, faceless figure engulfed by a towering, indiscriminate sky speaks as much to the idea of spiritual yearning as does any Bible passage or sermon. Like Ida Lupino's home in the center of the snow-covered valley in *On Dangerous Ground,* the image speaks of our essential isolation. Like Carl Theodor Dreyer, my grandfather was able to capture the landscape's innately religious aspect, both its grandeur and its menace, its eerie extension beyond the edge of the horizon, and its meaningless dispersal. And in that sense, my grandfather Selmer, the Lutheran pastor, the most sincerely religious person I knew, was the only person in the family capable of capturing this sense of hopeless resignation that circumscribes any attempt to find purpose in the world. The photograph speaks to me because its ostentatious austerity, its fascination with the unrelenting grayness of the heavens, and its emphasis on the insignificance of its human subject amid the boundless void of the physical world, together manifest a vision in which the hope of faith will always remain reined in.

§

I've been drawn to this photograph of my great-grandmother because she is searching, just as I am. We're always pursuing our origins — as if this need to seek is in our blood — but the deeper I've delved, the more I've come to recognize the fundamentally illusory nature of the concept of origins. The beginning we've been seeking, after all, has always been the conclusion to some earlier narrative other than our own. My great-grandmother was pointing spatially but also temporally — to her own earlier incarnation, but also, though she most likely wasn't actively considering it, to the age that preceded her own family's life on the prairie. She was trying to renew contact with her younger self, but she was also, even if only unconsciously, reaching out to absorb another story's aftershocks. And because I am a searcher just as she is, I have been reaching out as well. I have become curious, too. The more I've studied the photographs of my ancestors, the more I've wondered about which histories came to an end so that my family was able to begin its beginnings.

But my great-grandmother's methods intrigue me: unlike me, she's not looking back through old family photo albums, nor through the memories she'd been recycling for decades, but looking in the environment itself, in the land and the sky that envelop her, the same land and sky that captivated me just as powerfully when my family drove through the Great Plains back when I was young, the same land and sky that have captivated me yet again as I've been poring over images online of the sprawling Dakota terrain, the same placid domain watched over by the same clouds that my unconscious has arbitrarily settled on as the origin of my identity.

I used to think of this photograph as despairing, but lately I've begun to think of it more optimistically — perhaps because lately I've begun to see it not so much as an image of a woman pointing into an absence but as an image of a woman communing with the physical world. But as with all hermeneutic endeavors, my shifting understanding of the photograph says as much about me as it does about the picture itself. I imagine her these days as if she's bonding herself with her environment, I suspect, because my own interests have been drifting over the years more toward the natural world. The more I've become interested in New York's topography, its trees, birds, and waterways, the more I've felt a yearning to commune with the land and the sky myself.

While the notion that we might be able to think in league with the natural world strikes me sometimes as merely the vestige of ancient superstitions, I also like to consider sometimes whether it may not be as irrational as it seems. Over the last few decades, scientists have been studying how living beings that don't have brains — from bacteria to trees — demonstrate what we might call thinking behavior. While people may disagree whether other living entities are engaged in actual thinking, those disagreements typically depend merely on how people choose to define their terms. It's indisputable, though, that other living entities without brains can detect, sense, or perceive objects, beings, and events in the phenomenal world and change their behavior in response to what they've detected, sensed, or perceived. Trees, for example, can sense other objects in their path and then, over the course of years, grow around them. Trees can sense when a dangerous insect lands on one of its leaves and then send chemicals through their branches to that exact leaf to fight that specific type of insect. Trees can sense through underground fungal networks all the trees growing nearby; they can detect through those fungal networks which of those nearby trees belong to which species; they can sense whether those other trees need water; they can send water through those fungal connections to help other trees; and they usually decide to send more water to trees of their own species.

It only takes a slight shifting of perspective — or, perhaps, a non-rational leap of faith akin to the belief in God or the emotional submission to a work of art — to conceive of non-living entities as similarly exhibiting thinking behavior. The notion that rocks and soil, rivers and canyons, rolling hills and the endlessly unfolding plains are similarly able to engage in mental behavior admittedly seems implausible, if not absurd. And it is. Except that on some level we already believe that this is the case — at least on a semantic or metaphorical level. We use language that already hints at our non-rational acceptance of inorganic cognition. We say, for instance, that mountains feed plains, that rivers find channels, that forests renew themselves after fires, that ecosystems bring themselves into balance, that the planet itself is negotiating the needs and desires of its inhabitants or of its constituent components. This is, perhaps, merely linguistic shorthand, merely a poetic conceit. But the limited perceptual skills of the human animal make it impossible for us to detect or to even comprehend what thinking behavior might look like on a geological or atmospheric scale, if such a thing could possibly even exist. Our intellectual insufficiencies, though, are often the catalyst for more poetic modes of comprehension. We think in metaphors, after all, to overcome rationality's limitations.

Imagining that the land and the sky have intelligence is not rational, of course. But as with Carl Jung's idea that we've inherited our aesthetic values as autonomous complexes in the infrastructure of the unconscious, we sometimes consider the non-rational to be quite sensible precisely because the rational feels so inadequate or so cold. Our non-rational experience with art has productive benefits, after all, much like the non-rational practice of religious ritual. Devotional practice has utility, not truth. We rarely ask, after all, whether a work of art is "true." If anything, we submit ourselves to aesthetic experiences — artistic modes of thinking and of knowing — precisely so that we can overcome the stultifying dullness that an exclusively rational worldview would inevitably engender.

So sometimes I like to entertain the notion — regardless of whether I believe it might be even partially true — that the land and the sky exhibit intelligent behavior and that the earth and the heavens thus have consciousness. The idea that the land and the sky see us, know us, and understand us is, perhaps, merely the secular, metaphorical version of the religious superstition that God is watching over us from the heavens. But I find it a useful — or perhaps merely comforting — intellectual tool to imagine that the land and the sky have both conscious and unconscious aspects of mind, that they have knowledge, that they have their own needs and desires, that they harbor memories, some dimly remembered, some long forgotten and churning deep within, desperate to make themselves known once again in the minds of others. So I like to imagine — even though I don't exactly believe that it's true — that the memories of the land and the sky have found a way to embed themselves within me just as I like to imagine that the values of my ancestors have seeded themselves in my unconscious. And I like to think, therefore, that I am able to detect, sense, and perceive the memories of the earth and of the heavens just as I am able to come into contact with the aesthetic impulse of my lineage. The land and the sky must be wise: they have been here, after all, hundreds of millions of years longer than we have. Or at least the notion of their wisdom, like Jung's conception of the mind, resonates with some aspect of my personality. Its emotional utility is more important to me than its correctness. That being said, the non-rational, as useful as it may be, ultimately leaves us in a position of doubt, which is, in turn, a fundamental aspect of faith. So I've come to accept this hopeless hope as a productive strategy for flourishing — or perhaps, merely a defensive tactic for survival.

When I'm most susceptible to this kind of non-rational speculation, I begin to look at the photographs of my great-grandmother with new eyes. She's not despairing. No. She is wise. She is wise like the earth and the heavens are wise. Because the imagination unveils itself so often as a palliative, I like to imagine that my great-grandmother in that photograph is a conjurer: she's becoming one with space and time; she's knitting herself into the fabric of geological and celestial knowledge; she's absorbing memories from within the earth's interior and the atmosphere's invisible core. And she is channeling those memories to me.

§

I'd been drawn to an idea about my hard-scrabble Norwegian immigrant ancestors in the nineteenth-century Dakotas because the notion of a stoic resolve in the face of privation appealed to a necessarily heroic sense of self. But if I remove myself from the limited horizons of my own mind, if I imaginatively attempt to see from the land's and the sky's perspective, my family's history in the Great Plains becomes but a microscopic fleck amid the millennial flow of time. The story I've returned to again and again of my forebears moving into a vast, vacant, and unforgiving landscape is itself, of course, a myth. My great-grandparents and great-great-grandparents hadn't moved into virgin land, after all. My ancestors moved — as white settlers on the American frontier always had — into regions that had been emptied out over the preceding few centuries by disease, war, and forced relocation.

By the time they arrived in the Dakota Territory in the 1880s, plagues of smallpox, typhus, cholera, and measles had been coursing over the continent in wave after wave for almost four hundred years. The Indigenous population of the Western Hemisphere had fallen by more than 90% over the centuries since Christopher Columbus landed on Hispaniola in 1492, a loss of millions of human beings. And European immigrants in the United States had been pushing the Native Americans who'd survived ever westward, from the Atlantic coast toward the interior of the continent, generation after generation, for a quarter of a millennium.[1]

My ancestors moved into the Dakota Territory in the 1880s because the federal government had just recently opened those lands for white settlement. It was only at the tail end of the 1870s that the United States — after a few decades of fighting Indigenous people on the Plains and a coordinated effort to eradicate the bison from the American West — had finally forced the Mandan, Hidatsa, Arikara, Ojibwe, and the seven bands of the Sioux to retreat from their own lands and their own way of life and live instead in the shadows of white settlers on reservations that the United States government had assigned to them. My great-great-grandparents and their kin settled down on 160-acre allotments where Indigenous Americans had previously made their home. And though my ancestors, I'm sure, conveniently avoided thinking about these facts or passing them on to the next generation, it's impossible to erase these narratives from that environment.

---

1   Robert V. Hine and John Mack Faragher, *The American West: A New Interpretive History* (New Haven: Yale University Press, 2000), 27, and Charles C. Mann, *1491: New Revelations of the Americas Before Columbus* (New York: Alfred A. Knopf, 2005), 90–101.

Before my family's arrival at the end of the nineteenth century, the Lakota — the westernmost band of the Sioux — ruled the Great Plains, roaming from Minnesota to western Montana on horseback, following herds of bison, hunting with shotguns, and living in teepees. The Mandan, Hidatsa, and Arikara, meanwhile, lived in permanent villages along the banks of the Missouri River in earthen-mound lodges that they built out of timbre and mud, raising fields of beans, squash, and corn. And because they were the only sedentary tribes for hundreds of miles around, they served as the economic middlemen for trade between Indigenous people in the Rockies and the deserts of the Southwest and the Indigenous people to the north and on the eastern side of the Mississippi. The Ojibwe, meanwhile, flourished up north around the Great Lakes, living in temporary homes they called wigwams that they constructed out of fallen branches and leaves. They roamed throughout the seasons, gathering wild rice, hunting deer in the woods, fishing in the lakes, and trading beaver fur and bison robes from tribes in the west to the Canadian and American cities to the east.[2]

But in the century before that, every single one of these tribes followed a very different way of life. Before the eighteenth century, the Lakota and the other bands of the Sioux hadn't yet made it to the Great Plains. They didn't have guns; they hadn't yet seen horses; they didn't live in teepees; they didn't hunt bison. They lived, instead, among the lakes of Northern Minnesota, in the shadows of the more powerful Ojibwe up north, gathering wild rice, fishing in the lakes, hunting game, and traversing the waters in birch bark canoes. And in that era, the Ojibwe had reached their peak of political and economic influence in the region; they worked as the middlemen for British traders

2   Pekka Hämäläinen, *Lakota America: A New History of Indigenous Power* (New Haven: Yale University Press, 2019); Elizabeth A. Fenn, *Encounters at the Heart of the World: A History of the Mandan People* (New York: Hill and Wang, 2014); Anton Treuer, *Ojibwe in Minnesota* (St. Paul: Minnesota Historical Society Press, 2010); and David Treuer, *The Heartbeat of Wounded Knee: Native America from 1890 to the Present* (New York: Riverhead Books, 2019).

and the French traders who'd preceded them over the previous centuries, orchestrating a continent-wide trade in bison hides, beaver furs, and guns. And the Mandan, Hidatsa, and Arikara, much more populous than they became a century later, lived hundreds of miles to the south along the Missouri River.

But in the centuries before that, none of these tribes lived even close to the Great Plains. The Sioux and the Mandan originated much farther south, perhaps as remnants of the Mississippian civilizations that had built the great urban centers in the American Southeast so clearly inspired by the Mayan and Aztec cities of what is now Mexico. The Ojibwe, meanwhile, came from much farther east, most likely along the Atlantic coast, where other Algonquian-speaking people had lived for hundreds of years.

And we don't know who lived on the Great Plains in the centuries before that, or for the fifteen thousand years before that, after human beings first entered the Western Hemisphere. And we don't know what the land and the sky witnessed for eons before their arrival, or for the millions of years before the human animal emerged, as the continents drifted, just as clouds have always drifted, just as humans later migrated over the face of the earth, transforming both themselves and the land by colliding and breaking apart, just as the continents are still drifting, still transfiguring themselves, still yearning to become something other than they are.

If I understand my identity through the lens of my immigrant ancestors, I must also, then, see my character inextricably intertwined with the people who lived on the Plains before their arrival and, as well, with the people who preceded them. The aspect of my persona that embraces non-rational and aesthetic modes of thinking and knowing wants to believe that the earth's past has connected me to them. It's comforting to want to believe that we can somehow make sense of—even if we can never rectify—the traumas of the past; it feels healthy to think that we can gain access to other people's lives, to their narratives and perspectives, by divining the invisible essence of the environment that connects us. The land and the sky, I like to think — because such imaginings bear with them an aesthetic and spiritual utility — harbor memories of my immigrant ancestors' predecessors. If we bend down and put our ear to the ground and listen to the rumblings of the earth, if we raise our eyes and stare intently into the distance to decode the cryptic language of the heavens, we might begin to resuscitate those dormant memories and make them intelligible once again.

Perhaps that was what my great-grandmother was ultimately trying to accomplish by standing in that empty field, pointing off into the emptiness of the distance: like a wizened necromancer, she was conjuring ghosts, listening to the soil and the grasses and communing with the invisible interior of the atmosphere in order to reanimate the dead. Unleashing those repressed, primordial memories from the geological and celestial unconscious might possibly nurture a rapport with those who preceded her. Imagining her image in this way, as with all religious or poetic practice, exercises our innate metaphorical impulses in order to inhabit the full breadth and depth of our potential humanity. Conceiving of ourselves as fundamentally intertwined with the physical history of the earth gives us a sense of the ecstatic reach of geological and celestial time, engendering our innate capacities to understand and thus to become one with infinity.

And this faint brush with eternity reinforces our recognition of the incessant evolution in both the external world and the core of the inner self. We have been drifting just as the land has been drifting. We have been rupturing, torn asunder, just as the clouds have been. But the land where my mothers and fathers lived and gave birth to my sense of my origins has witnessed far-reaching and violent transformations over the last few centuries: civilizations have come and gone, come and gone, swept aside by the tides of history. The Great Plains has undergone a constant, sweeping metamorphosis catalyzed by disease and wars and invasions and economic upheavals. The Great Plains over the last several hundred years has been the site of continuous annihilation. Death and destruction. Pestilence and extermination. The only thing permanent in the land has been impermanence itself. Annihilation, in fact, has been the lifeblood of this environment. And this annihilating evolution, then, must have seeped into me as well, must have become an essential aspect of my character, one of the fundamental structuring absences of my identity.

§

As I've been poring over the images of my family's past over the last few years, I've felt myself drawn, tentatively but inexorably, as if tethered by some invisible thread, to more and more images whose ostensible otherness has been striking unexpected chords within me as well: images of the inhabitants of the Great Plains who preceded my ancestors, men and women who appear, on the surface, as distant from me as the obverse faces of the moon might seem to each other. But the more I've studied their portraits, the more I've felt that thread tightening, as if the earth's memory has been pulling me in, reminding me over and over of our inextricable interdependence — or perhaps merely of our yearning for that interdependence, for the actualization of our mutual resemblance, of our metaphysical mirroring.

Besides the photographs of my great-grandparents and great-great-grandparents, the images that have compelled me most intensely over the last few years are three portraits painted by the Swiss and American artists Karl Bodmer and George Catlin of the Mandan leader Mato-Topé — or, Four Bears — who lived from 1784 to 1837 in the village of Mih-tutta-hang-kusch along the northern banks of the Missouri River, just a two-hour drive from where my mother grew up in what is now North Dakota.

In my favorite, an 1833 watercolor by Bodmer — a much more talented artist than the more-famous Catlin — Mato-Topé stands alert, staring confidently off into the distance, holding a red tomahawk in a scabbard of blue and white mollusk shells tightly in both hands (fig. 10). He has an aquiline nose. His mouth is resolutely firm. He's painted his face the color of aged tallow or maybe an ashen ochre, with a red oval around his right eye, a red band along the base of the right side of his chin and forehead, and a yellow line along the left. He's painted his chest

Fig. 10. Karl Bodmer (Swiss, 1809–1893), *Mató-Tópe, Mandan Chief,* 1834, watercolor and graphite on paper. Joslyn Art Museum, Omaha, Nebraska, Gift of the Enron Art Foundation, 1986.49.26. Photograph © Bruce M. White, 2019.

with red streaks from his neck to his belly, like gouges or scratch marks or the creased trunk of a great red oak, but he's left one ghostly, pale mustard hand print untouched above his left chest, a sign, he explained to Bodmer, that he'd taken prisoners in battle. He's made his hair up into a tangled crown, with a tuft of yellow owl feathers in a knot at the back of his head, a sheaf of eagle feathers pointing to the sky from whence they came, six wooden sticks that mark each of the bullet wounds he'd received in battle, and a wooden knife hanging above his right ear as the visible memory of the time he killed a Cheyenne chief in combat.[3]

In Bodmer's second portrait, Mato-Topé stands erect, proud, wearing a grand, knee-length robe made from the hide of a bighorn sheep and a resplendent headdress made with dozens of eagle feathers — topped by a pair of bison horns — that drapes down his back almost to the ground. He lifts his chin, staring confidently off into the distance, holding a pike in one hand. He's painted his face for this occasion with vertical streaks of chocolate brown outlined with blood-red slashes. He puffs up his chest to show off his robe's design: a red and blue isosceles triangle on a field of bright canary yellow.

Mato-Topé poses only in his finest, ceremonial raiment, presenting himself as a noble and accomplished warrior, partly because he wanted his Mandan peers to recognize him in that role, partly because he wanted the outside world to understand him as this persona, but also partly because Bodmer — as Catlin had done just one year earlier — asked him to portray himself in his most striking battle vestments for an American and European audience that the artist knew was yearning for an exoticized image. The leader of Bodmer's ethnographic expedition, the German aristocrat Prince Alexander Philipp Maximilian zu Wied-Neuwied, recalled how eager the Mandan were to have their portraits painted, how proud they were to parade their varied and elaborate apparel for their foreign visitors. So Mato-Topé and Bodmer collaborated in creating these images just as my ancestors had collaborated with the photographers who'd orchestrated the poses that they willingly performed. And Mato-Topé, like my ancestors, knowingly and willingly invented this vision of himself — partly as truth, partly as fiction — dram-

---

3   Maximilian zu Wied, *People of the First Man: Life Among the Plains Indians in Their Final Days of Glory: The Firsthand Account of Prince Maximilian's Expedition Up the Missouri River, 1833–34,* eds. Davis Thomas and Karin Ronnefeldt, watercolors by Karl Bodmer (New York: E.P. Dutton, 1976), 192, 202–3.

atizing a more eminent and heroic version of himself than he inhabited in his everyday life. Like them, he was fashioning an identity to be handed down to his descendants, stamping his mark on the imagination of the future.

I've studied Mato-Topé's image with the same fascination I've studied the photographs of my great-great-great-great-grand-parents Andreas and Olea Lundene, my great-great-grandfather Moses Flugekvam, my great-great-grandparents John Caspar and Louise Hummel, and my great-grandparents Stener and Gertrude Hilde. His image compels me because I sometimes like to think — though I know that these images cannot reveal any truths about either my ancestors or about him — that perhaps my spectatorial devotion might revive some spiritual remnant of the past that adhered itself to our shared environment. As if gazing over the surface of a river might unveil the occulted color of the sky. As if studying smoke in a mirror might reveal the essence of flame's interior.

I'm drawn to him because his image is a manifestation of the structuring absence of my origins. The Mandan lived in the region near where my ancestors settled in the Dakotas in the 1870s and 1880s, a mere half-century after Mato-Topé presented himself for Bodmer's contemplation. I'm drawn to him because the forced relocation of his people — and of the other Indigenous people of the Plains — made my very existence possible.

I'm drawn to him also because of the allure of the image itself. His personality is so forceful, so vibrantly excessive, I want his spirit to redound upon the world that I inhabit today. I'm drawn to him because he is a spectral force — partly of his own invention, partly of Bodmer's, and partly of my own. Like Gena Rowlands, he's made of his body an emblem of visionary excess, the visible antithesis to my ascetic notions about my identity.

And I am not alone in being fascinated with him. Catlin visited Mih-tutta-hang-kusch over the winter of 1832 to 1833, during one of his five painting expeditions throughout the West, and chose Mato-Topé as his favorite subject, finding in him an inescapable magnetism, referring to him as "the most popular man in the nation."[4] Bodmer, meanwhile, visited him just one year later and found himself equally drawn in by the chief's charisma, painting him more than any other figure he met on the expedition. And Prince Maximilian zu Wied mentions him more than any other Native American he met on his journey, calling him an "eminent man… possessing many fine and noble traits of character."[5]

But Mato-Topé's romanticized vision of this heroic Mandan identity was the product of multiple forces: it was inextricably bound up — as it was for my forebears — with the territory where he lived, with that floridly flat stretch of the continent, but also with the economic systems and cultural assumptions of the Europeans and Americans for whom he was posing. His imagination about his own identity was both cultivated and constrained by international affairs that had been bringing rapid change to the continent's interior over the preceding two centuries — for the Indigenous and the white populations at roughly the same speed. He was, in his own mind, performing an authentic, if somewhat embellished, Mandan identity, but his notions of Mandan identity — like notions about any ethnicity — were the product of other cultures beyond his control.

The red steel blade that he holds in one portrait came, most likely, from Americans working for the fur companies at the forts along the Missouri River that John Jacob Astor had been operating since 1808, the same kind of axe that his own ancestors previously procured from British traders a century earlier and from French traders a century before that. His earrings and the decorative handle of his axe are made from mollusk shells that he acquired from Indigenous traders to the West who acquired them from other Indigenous traders from over the Rockies on the Pacific Coast. The knife he wore in his hair was patterned on those produced by American blacksmiths back east. Even his bighorn robe came from an animal shot with the kind of gun that his grandparents' generation never would have seen.

---

4   Fenn, *Encounters at the Heart of the World,* 302.

5   zu Wied, *People of the First Man,* 192.

So in fashioning this image of himself, Mato-Topé was very consciously presenting what he knew to be a composite identity: one culture, he was indicating, was always an intricate and fabulous mesh of every neighboring culture and, indeed, of every culture spanning the entire continent.

Mato-Topé aimed to develop this idealized rendition of himself even further: in addition to being the most captivating muse of the Great Plains, he was also — perhaps not coincidentally, given the strength of his personality — one of the region's most eminent artists himself. Like many Plains tribes, the Mandan, too, had taken up the practice known as "winter counts": pictographic narratives of a tribe's past that their designated artist-historians painted on the back of bison hides and handed down from generation to generation. During the long, snow-bound winters, the artist-historian of any given band would add one image to a long line of images that represented the single most important event for that clan over the preceding year. Then, every year in the depths of winter, the community would gather round and listen to the painter-chronicler narrate their shared history back to them — image by image, year by year — for dozens, sometimes more than a hundred years back. The tribes, then, conceived of their winter counts as genre-crossing, multimedia entities and performances, since the pictographs functioned simultaneously as visual artworks on their own and as mnemonic devices that helped the artist narrate a history to a gathering of like-minded souls, making the process as much oral and communal as it was pictorial.[6] So it was not at all surprising that Mato-Topé felt drawn to the paintings of Catlin and Bodmer; his European visitors, after all, were merely engaging in the same artistic practice, with a slightly different formal agenda, that he'd been engaging in himself for years.

6   Cristina E. Burke, "Waniyetu Wówapi: An Introduction to the Lakota Winter Count Tradition," in *The Years the Stars Fell: Lakota Winter Counts at the Smithsonian,* eds. Candace S. Greene and Russell Thornton (Washington, DC: The Smithsonian Institution, 2007), 1–11.

Mato-Topé thus saw in Bodmer a kindred spirit. They were both artists, both visionaries. Soon he was sharing his own art with his new friend from Switzerland, drawing on Mandan aesthetic traditions to offer up a complementary vision of himself to pair with the portrait on which he'd already collaborated with Bodmer. As both artist and muse, subject and seer — one of the most significant artistic figures of the nineteenth-century American West — Mato-Topé was, like all of us, crafting a vision of himself through images and the narratives that those images hinted at, stories and identities that were, by their very nature, always a creative mixture of fact and fiction. And like my grandfather Selmer taking photographs of his mother lost in a sea of grass, or like me writing about those very images that my grandfather produced, he was using art to synthesize his cultural past for the benefit of the future.

His own self-portraits speak back to us in an aesthetic language radically different from Bodmer's: instead of a realistic depiction of the physical form, his pictures aim for a more metaphysical understanding of their subject. Mato-Topé envisioned himself in a style that reminds me today of modernist abstraction, as if he needed to create a non-rational visual counterpart to Bodmer's rational conception of him as the only means of rendering the depth and multiplicity of his character. And this is, perhaps, one reason why his self-portraits resonate so deeply with me, with my own sense of the shifting and immaterial nature of the self. He saw himself as pure phantom, unconstrained by either Mandan society's or white society's pre-existing conceptions of what an individual might possibly be. He offered up a vision of identity radically different from that of my ancestors because, unlike them, he was able to perceive — or to dream up — a purely symbolic self that transgressed the bounds of his own biography, family, and culture, beyond the physical limitations of the land and the mental confines of time.

In my favorite of his own watercolors, he represents himself as an iconic, otherworldly force: his eyes are hollow, navy-blue circles shooting red triangles out like vectors of electric blood; his chin, too, is just one smeared red triangle (fig. 11). The right

Fig. 11. Attributed to Mató-Tópe (Mandan, c. 1775–1837), *Mató-Tópe: Self Portrait; holding a feather-covered shield, with a pair of ceremonial lances thrust into the ground,* c. 1833, watercolor on paper, Joslyn Art Museum, Omaha, Nebraska. Gift of the Enron Art Foundation, 1986.49.318.

side of his chest is red, the left a burnished gold. His legs are dashes of multi-colored horizontal lines, like weightless speed itself. He wears a flowing ceremonial headdress of perfectly geometrical and monochromatic eagle feathers that falls below his knees. He holds a flat blue shield ornamented with black and white triangles that mirror the feathers of his headdress. And he shares this almost entirely blank, otherworldly two-dimensional space with three ceremonial staffs that stand, against the logic of physics, like mythic totems of his interior energy.

To my mind, Mato-Topé understands himself — not as Bodmer or Catlin did, as mere exteriority, as mere man — but, more perceptively in his own mind, as a combination of exterior and interior, as man and spirit, because he knows that he belongs equally to the earthen-mound villages on the northern banks of the Missouri River, to the auspicious expanse of the Great Plains, and to the infinite wind that sweeps over the grasses, wind that is the inquisitive, caressing hand of the unbounded sky. The self, to him, is pure idea. He pictures this avatar of his identity, after all, standing in an abstract void that recalls, to my mind, the dingy pallor that Joan Mitchell made the background of her earliest canvases or the barely-swirling, ivory-cream aching emptiness that Cy Twombly liked to stab through with fragmentary bursts of iridescence.

And yet, as with the photographs of my great-grandparents and great-great-grandparents, as much as I am entranced, I am equally estranged. Mato-Topé's vision is as unfathomable as the image of my great-grandmother standing in the middle of that vast and empty field in the center of the vast and empty Plains, searching in vain. But this estrangement can be simultaneously liberating and disquieting. When we study any image, we always, inevitably, imbue that picture with our own concerns as much as we draw out the artist's or the subject's intentions. Studying images from the past like these that we hope might help explain ourselves back to ourselves is thus a hopelessly circular endeavor: we read into them what we believe the artists and subjects were expressing, yet we simultaneously see in them our own ideals, which we suspect have become our ideals, ironically, precisely because the subjects of the images have already bequeathed them to us. The process is always a twisted game, always an act of abandoning the self by re-articulating the self, always simultaneously an affirmation and repudiation.

We exoticize others because we necessarily exoticize ourselves. My exegesis of Mato-Topé surely would not jibe with how he must have seen his own identity, but with how I want — or need — to see a possibility of my own identity in him, to bring to life the potential for human connection. But the meanings of his images are multifaceted, fugitive. Even in the more traditional portraits by Catlin and Bodmer, multiple forces of meaning are intertwining. We simultaneously see how Catlin and Bodmer saw him, how they wanted to present themselves as artists to an Eastern cultural elite, how Mato-Topé wanted to present himself to both the Mandan world and the white world, and how we ourselves want or need to see him today. And his own more radical presentation of his persona is even more complex since his self-portrait's manifold meanings are the product of his conversations with, but also against, those preceding representations. Thus, the image that any of us construct for ourselves must be equally multifaceted, equally the product of ourselves and of others — an identity, then, that we can never fully comprehend on our own.

We will never know, of course, how Mato-Topé might have interpreted his own images — either as subject or artist. He died just a few years after Catlin and Bodmer had befriended him. In 1837, in the last and most deadly wave of epidemics that spread through the Great Plains over the centuries since Columbus's arrival, the Mandan nation was decimated: almost 90% of its population — including Mato-Topé, his wives, and all his children — died in that single year.[7]

And that fact, too, casts a shadow over his images, just as it casts a shadow over the photograph of my great-grandmother. It suffuses my exegeses with a fatalistic impulse as well as the resulting need to transcend that very inclination. Thus, to my mind, Mato-Topé's watercolors evoke the same desperate need I see in the image of my great-grandmother pointing into the abyss, the same need I see in myself and in everyone, the need to search for that which cannot be found, the need to puncture the unrelenting desert exodus of the dying heavens.

As I did when looking at the photograph of my great-great-great grandfather Moses Flugekvam, I gaze intently into Mato-Topé's eyes. I try to pierce through them, to bring myself into contact with some churning interior. But his eyes are mere circles, more absence than presence. Nothing can escape their sunken gravity. They cannot possibly speak to me as much as my soul wants them to. Nor can I possibly speak back to them.

7   Fenn, *Encounters at the Heart of the World,* 319–25.

The Sky :: Annihilation

These days, now comfortably middle-aged, my infrequent expeditions to and from the revival houses in New York no longer feel as exhilarating as they once did. When I was young, I started going to the movies to inhabit a kind of mental sophistication in contrast to the worldview of my provincial adolescence. But by now I've lived inside that persona for a quarter of a century. I've seen so many movies at this point — thousands upon thousands of them — that it's become harder and harder to make the discoveries I once hoped would change me. Obsessively seeking out artistic experiences, it turns out, reduces the possibility of experiencing any further aesthetic epiphanies. I can no longer feel that revelatory flash that I felt with the auteurs and actors of my youth. My inveterate artistic curiosity eventually nurtured its own obsolescence.

These days, my filmic experience is, more often than not, a circling back or inward, a reflection on some past glory whose spark has faded. My new discoveries, when I do have them, tend to be minor films I never managed to see during my first great sweep of the canon. But even the experience of falling in love with a new discovery feels muted now: like an animal in some odd Pavlovian experiment, I've become desensitized to the very experience that once brought me joy. Now when I see movies, I feel as if my unconscious is merely re-affirming a known quantity, continually burnishing the treasure chest I'd planted at the bottom of the sea. But this continual traversing through the familiar is the very antithesis of the spirit of reinvention: I can no longer use movies as I once did to define my identity diametrically against my past.

The first year of the pandemic only intensified this sense of stultification. I went more than a year without entering a movie theater, the longest absence since I was a child. And that year without movies extended my leisurely drift away from the cinema into what now seems like what might have been a clean break. But since the innate yearning for reinvention never fades, it's become clear to me that the best way that I can redefine myself these days is by turning my back on my earlier cinephile identity.

I look back now at that younger incarnation with a sense of bemusement, only partially recognizing the person I used to be. Growing older confirms the suspicions of youth: with hindsight, one can see that the self is always drifting and receding, like a cloud, always in a process of transformation, surging and collapsing, dissipating now and then beyond the horizon of consciousness. Until it becomes mere memory. Yet the disintegration of a cloud is illusory since clouds always return, rising from their ocean cemeteries to reimagine themselves anew, undulating and billowing, drifting over the land as witnesses once again only so that they can recede, dissipate, and disappear in their cyclical return to the seas. It's true that there's no such thing as a cloud. But it's also true that we'll always continue to believe in them.

This book is a memoir, but like every memoir it's the story of a person who never quite existed, a collage of fractured memories, retrospective shames and desires, a fictive reassembling. It's a reflection on a hybrid character who surfaced during that brief window when the need to form an identity had reached its most fevered intensity. Indeed, this memoir is an examination not so much of anyone's life at all, but of a particular psychic interior that needed to make itself known.

We are always seeking, but the searching in our adulthood is propelled by the same paradox that inspired the searching of our youth. The process of self-making is always circular, always a return as much as it is an escape. So it's not surprising that even today, feeling an uncontrollable need to distance myself from my cinephile youth, I nevertheless feel an equally uncontrollable need to cast my gaze deeper and deeper back from where I came. The centrifugal force that looks outward and forward, away from the past, inevitably catalyzes its centripetal counterpoint, making us look inward and backward once again.

These days, my desire for redefinition has been revealing itself not so much in artistic but in physical form. These days I often find myself wandering — on foot or on bicycle — on long, meandering excursions, mapping my sense of my identity onto the city's landscape, its hills and flatlands, its streets and intersections, its rivers and bridges. In these restorative peregrinations, I'm not quite exploring, not quite drifting, maybe just taking up time, as if my conscious mind has been pushing me out into the world, but my unconscious mind has been shepherding my inquisitive aimlessness.

On Saturday and Sunday mornings, especially, I tend to get lost. I take the subway to some random destination, then just start walking, who knows where. Or more often I go out on long bike rides with no destination in mind. My only goal, it seems, is to get out of the house, which is a way of getting away from myself. I need to orient my body in some new direction, transport it into unfamiliar locations in order to untether myself through time in an aleatory flow. So I ride, from neighborhood to neighborhood, up and down hills, unaware of where I'm going or why, floating across the city through its various microenvironments, its ascents and descents, hoping to coax my persona to shift and morph, to billow and recede, and to transform itself once again.

The other day, I rode my bike from where I now live out in central Brooklyn — a few miles farther out than I did back in my heroic age of cinephilia, the consequence of a city that keeps evolving, that keeps on buckling in on itself, then distending — to roam on an hours-long ride that took me, for reasons that were unclear to me, over several of the most iconic bridges that connect the outer boroughs to Manhattan, riding up into Queens, then crossing the East River over the Queensboro Bridge and back, down into Brooklyn to cross the Williamsburg Bridge and back, down to the Manhattan Bridge to cross over and back, and finally over the Brooklyn Bridge — one of the paradigmatic images of the city, the longest suspension bridge in the world and the tallest man-made structure in the Western Hemisphere back when it was finally completed in 1884 — and came to a stop finally on the wooden promenade at the base of one of its two twin towers, the bridge's highest point, to gaze down into the churning waters of the East River below.

The river itself is never a singular entity, either. The waters from up north course down the Hudson River into the East River, then New York Bay, while salt water from the Atlantic Ocean pushes itself up through New York Bay, then into the East River, so that what we're witnessing is always an evolution, flowing up or flowing out, estuary or river, it's never entirely clear. It's always reforming itself just like the clouds I can sometimes glimpse reflected in its slate-grey waves and sunburnt crests. Perhaps it's not a river at all; perhaps there's no such thing as a river; perhaps there's only continual transformation, versatility and process, malleability and oscillation.

Gazing into the roiling currents below, exhausted from my long ride, my mind kept circling back to one of the films I loved most intensely back in my most obsessive days of youthful moviegoing. For some reason that day I kept thinking about *Only Angels Have Wings* from 1939, directed by Howard Hawks, one of my favorite auteurs. It's a movie about flight and suicide, about joy and oblivion, about people trying and failing to escape their pasts.

It's a movie about pilots who keep flying up into the air to escape the darkness of the earth, but in this movie, flight isn't a mode of poetic liberation. In this movie, the sky is even darker than the earth: it's always bleakly uninviting, marred by thunderstorms the desolate shades of gunflint and ash. And flying is dangerous. Because this movie is about the impossibility of rein-vention. The pilots keep crashing, injuring themselves, dying. By the end of the film everyone is either dead or has barely escaped death. But they keep on flying. The sky, it seems, is a strange compulsion. They keep on escaping the darkness of the earth so that they can exist, however briefly, in the darkness of the heavens — only so that they can return to the darkness of the earth once again.

And I, too, keep circling back and returning, then circling back and returning again. There's something about the movie that speaks to me — or, perhaps it's that there's something that's been slumbering within that the movie keeps energizing and releasing: an autonomous complex, some innate yearning that needs to surface, chords within me that need to vibrate now and then, compelling me to keep reenacting this experience, this gleefully cynical meditation on the defining paradox between conscious reimagination and unconscious adherence to the past, the irresolvable circularity that propels the characters' ecstatic despair, the very same tensions I imagined I was witnessing in the agitated waters beneath the bridge hundreds of feet below.

Our guide into this movie's mixed-up world of joyful nihilism is the female half of the couple whose possible romance moti-vates the narrative: Jean Arthur is our stand-in, our own vehicle for the search of identity, since she is so obviously reinventing herself anew from the moment she first enters the scene. She plays Bonnie, a Brooklyn showgirl who's been drifting through life, unmoored, who finds herself in the opening sequence step-ping off a boat into a dreary port town in South America that's hemmed in by a foggy ocean on one side and a range of tower-ing, craggy mountains on the other. Looking for a place to stay over for the night, she arrives at the film's epicenter, its only real setting, a dimly lit bar-restaurant-flophouse that's also a strug-gling airline outfit run by a charismatically amoral character named Geoff, the film's true star, Cary Grant.

The pilots there under his command are barely surviv-ing. They carry the mail over the mountains, but they couldn't explain why. It's not a real vocation. There's barely any money or pleasure in it. The job is not a real job, but a metaphor for oblivion. And the place they've chosen to live is a nowhere place — all shabby chiaroscuro — a symbolic anti-home for a group of men who've abandoned life to move to this outer edge of civilization where they've invented a moral system antithetical to the ethos that they all chose to leave behind.

In just a few minutes after she arrives on the scene, Bonnie meets a pilot named Joe who gets called up for a flight, loses himself in the pitch-black fog, comes crashing down into the earth, and dies in an explosive ball of flame.

Bonnie stumbles back into the dimly lit bar-restaurant-flophouse that she only now understands is a staging ground for an aerial form of Russian Roulette, the temporary holding pattern for a group of men who harbor a suicidal death wish they're unable to admit out loud, either to others or to themselves. Then the cook comes out from the kitchen carrying the steak that was supposed to be Joe's dinner — the very steak he'd promised to share with Bonnie upon his return — and asks who wants it. No one even blinks. Geoff takes the plate without a thought and greedily digs in. And Bonnie — aghast — objects. After all, she exclaims, that's Joe's steak. But the men, without missing a beat, answer her in well-practiced unison: "Who's Joe?"[1]

She stares back, indignant. But then, slowly, moment by moment, she becomes intrigued.

Who are these men, she begins to wonder, who've abandoned the world as we know it so that they can live only in the present, untethered to the past, who take flight, night after night, to free themselves, escaping the bonds of the earth, making their only home in this psychic threshold of the atmosphere? (fig. 12).

From that moment, Bonnie and Geoff's deepening flirtation propels the plot forward, a romance that blooms — as it does in almost every Hawks film — as the female lead earns the male star's respect by proving that she's every bit as tough as he is. Eventually, Geoff does come to admire her — because

---

1   Howard Hawks, dir., *Only Angels Have Wings* (Columbia Pictures, 1939; New York: Criterion Collection, 2016), Blu-Ray disc, 27:18–27:56.

Fig. 12. Screenshot from *Only Angels Have Wings* (dir. Howard Hawks, 1939).

she reminds him of himself—but he never bends her way. He keeps flying. Every night he takes off up into a sky whose seething clouds make a mockery of any dreams he might harbor for salvation.

But this way of life is a suicidal endeavor. Another pilot dies in the air. Geoff has an accident and almost dive bombs into the earth. Another gets his hands and face burned by flames from his engine. And Geoff's best friend dies as his plane hurtles through a rainstorm violently into the ground before the eyes of the entire company who've rushed outside to witness what they know will be his sudden, violent death in a fiery explosion, the very spectacle of their own self-annihilating desires. By the end of the movie, half of the pilots are dead, injured, or psychologically broken. But they keep on flying the mail over the mountains. The odds of survival for these men are so bad, one begins to suspect that they've never been trying to liberate themselves at all. On the contrary. It seems, instead, that they're all just waiting for the inevitable, playing out what Bonnie has come to call a crazy philosophy — each of them secretly wanting to die, but too afraid to admit it, biding their time before their passive commitment to suicide finally comes to fruition.

It is this darkness that initially brought me to the film. This vision of escape that was only a vision of death appealed to me back then for the same reasons that Béla Tarr's leaden skies did. But I kept returning to the film, I think — kept on being seduced into its fold — because its despair was inextricably intertwined with the joy and affection that this ragtag community had created for itself. The men Bonnie meets at this crazy staging ground for death, after all, are some of the happiest people she's ever met. That first night after Joe dies, every member of that small group gathers around a piano and takes out their guitars, trumpets, and maracas so they can belt out a few impromptu tunes together. Singing at the top of their lungs, they are bursting with cheer because they are living only in the moment, unburdened by the past, totally free in this mixed-up utopia that they've invented for themselves. And Bonnie's curiosity about this crazy philosophy of life is my curiosity, too. It is this exuberant grasp of life in the face of utter darkness to which I keep circling back.

Geoff, too, keeps on circling, keeps on trying to revive this spirit, keeps on returning to the sky, keeps on pushing himself mercilessly through the steps of his exuberantly nihilistic creed: every night, he takes himself up into the swirling storm clouds that are always there in order to free himself from the burdens of the earth. And every dawn he returns once again to Bonnie, by now his mirror image in her embrace of this meaningless existence, who helps nurture their shared commitment to this monomaniacal lifestyle of circling, this shared love for the churning clouds of the night sky that offer no escape. But every morning, when he sees her and thus comes into contact with the possibility for redemption once again, he knows that he must escape once more, up into the air, up into this abyss of the heavens, waiting for the inevitable moment when his inexorable returning will finally come to an end.

I know why the film speaks to me. I'm drawn into its orbit because of its cynicism and despair, its charcoal-gray, funereal skies, its suicidal hopelessness, but also because of its euphoric dissolution, its joyful flouting of conventions, its bonhomie and camaraderie, and its tender affection between men. And I'm drawn to it because, as always, in its cinematic splendor — its nighttime shadows, its circling narrative, its reshaping and ordering of space and time, and Cray Grant's charismatic sublimity — it reminds me of the overwhelming power of the movies, which are still so much larger and so much more perfect than real life. I'm drawn to it because it's about the need to escape the past, but also about the inevitable need to return, and about the idea of love as the only possible antidote to this ceaseless circling, this irreconcilable conflict between our histories that made us and our attempts at emancipation.

§

We tend to ascribe a comforting coherence to our ancestry: it is the root from which we grew. And roots by their very nature, we like to think, must be stable, moored beyond our perceptual capabilities in the rich loam of the earth. But the past, in fact, has always churned with a self-annihilating streak. Every past generation, after all, was merely a future that a particular culture had invented in contradistinction to the generations that had preceded it. Thus, the past is always intrinsically bound up in self-destruction; self-destruction, we might say, is the past's very essence.

My own link to history is no different. Almost everyone who came before me in my mythic imaginings about my origins, I've come to learn, refused to lay down roots, but lived out, instead, a typical American mode of living, continually migrating, picking up stakes, and reinventing themselves. In this, they were no different than the Ojibwe, Sioux, Mandan, Hidatsa, and Arikara who had preceded and coexisted with them, who have always been on the move, evolving over the centuries, and who have themselves, over the millennia, replaced other cultures that preceded them. My ancestors' continual relocations throughout the nineteenth and twentieth centuries was the norm, not the exception. We tend to think of transience as a modern, urban phenomenon, with cities as the prototypical symbol of a roiling evolution, but farmers in America have always been at the forefront of geographic reinvention. Ever since the first generation of Europeans settled in Massachusetts and Virginia in the early 1600s, their children have always moved on — north and south and west — over the Appalachians into the Northwest Territory, forcing the native inhabitants of those lands ever westward, generation after generation, ingesting the continent in a few deep breaths. Out on the Plains, reinvention was the dominant mode of living, which made dissolution and ruination the region's driving force. As I've been researching my family's past, studying census records and land sale documents and city directories, I've been struck time and again by how difficult it is to locate the homes where my ancestors used to live. Virtually none of those houses, in fact, are still standing today.

If my great-grandmother Gertrude Hilde had managed to travel back in time to her own family's roots in Story City, Iowa, where she was born and raised, she would've found that the farm where she and her parents lived from 1873 to 1885 was no longer there. The home where her husband Stener Hilde first lived in Lyle, Minnesota, with his parents and brothers between 1877 and 1880, is no longer there. The farmhouse where Stener's parents, Anders Hansen Hilde and Randi Olsdatter Hilde, moved after Stener and his brothers got married and left home, standing just outside the town of Jack Creek in Emmett County, Iowa, is no longer there. The three farmhouses where Stener's brothers, Roy, Hans, and Ole lived near him in Walworth County, South Dakota, from 1881 to 1902 — just a few miles from the Missouri River, directly across the water from the Great Sioux Reservation, which Congress had divided up into even smaller reservations over those decades — are no longer there. The farmhouse where Stener and Gertrude Hilde lived outside the town of Donalda in Alberta, Canada, from 1902 to 1938 and where my grandfather Selmer was born and raised is no longer there.

The farmhouse in Dane County, Wisconsin, where my great-great-great-grandparents Andreas and Olea Lundene lived with their children from 1850 until the 1870s is no longer there. The farmhouses where their daughter Ingbor Lundene lived with her husband Ole Thorsten Jeglum in Floyd County, Iowa, from 1874 to his death in 1889, is no longer there; the farmhouse where Ole Thorsten Jeglum had first lived in Dane County, Wisconsin, back in the 1860s is no longer there; the farmhouse where Ingbor Lundene lived with her daughter Olina and Olina's husband in Mitchell County, Iowa, from 1890 to 1919 is no longer there; the farmhouse where she lived with her daughter Tillie and Tillie's husband in McCone, Montana, from 1920 to 1929 is no longer there; the house where she retired with Tillie and her son-in-law in Long Beach, California, is no longer there.

The farmhouse in Walsh County, North Dakota, where my great-great-grandparents Moses and Zahanna Flugekvam lived from 1884 to 1917 is no longer there. The farmhouse where their daughter, my great-grandmother Nellie Flugekvam lived with her husband Henry Otis Jeglum outside the town of Fairdale in Walsh County, North Dakota, from 1900 to 1950 is no longer there. My grandmother Ina Jeglum Hilde grew up on that farm in the 1910s and 1920s, but all that is there now is shorn, empty fields as far as the eye can see.

The farmhouse where my great-great-great grandparents Lars Ringdahl and his wife Mette Jensen Ringdahl moved in 1882 in Aliceton Township, Ransom County, North Dakota, is no longer there. The farmhouse where their daughter Alice lived in Ransom County with her husband Ole Melby from their marriage in 1893 to his death in 1918 is no longer there. The farmhouse where my great-great-great-grandparents Christian Jorgenson and Mary Sorensen Jorgenson lived in Freeborn County, Minnesota, from 1881 to 1894 is no longer there; the farmhouse where they lived in Winnebago County, Iowa, from 1895 to 1904 is no longer there; the farmhouse where they lived in Sargent County, North Dakota, from 1905 through the 1920s is no longer there.

The farmhouse where my great-great-great-grandparents Johann and Cathrina Bubach lived in La Moure County, just outside of Litchville, North Dakota, from 1883 to 1915 is no longer there. The farmhouse just down the road where their daughter Maria Bubach lived with her husband, my great-great-grandfather Heinrich Karl Dibbern from 1885 to 1926 is no longer there.

The building where my great-great-grandfather John Caspar Hummel attended Lutheran Seminary in Mendota, Illinois, between 1888 and 1892 is no longer there; the parsonage where he lived in Webster, South Dakota, with his wife Louise between 1893 and 1898 is no longer there; the farmhouse where her parents, my great-great-great-grandparents Ferdinand and Johanna Schwandt lived outside Big Stone City, South Dakota, from 1891 to 1898 is no longer there; the parsonage where John Caspar and Louise Schwandt Hummel lived just outside of Litchville in LaMoure County, North Dakota, between 1899 and John Caspar's death in 1922 is no longer there. I can find the empty space on Google Maps where the parsonage once stood, where my great uncle and step-grandfather Heinie grew up only because the church is still there. But beside that church there is nothing, nothing but empty space.

Even in my parents' generation, homes have been impermanent and extinguishable, diaphanous and conceptual. Surprisingly, most of the houses that even my parents knew in their generation are no longer there. The farmhouse where my mother's father grew up in Alberta, Canada is no longer there. The farmhouse where my mother's mother grew up outside of Fairdale, North Dakota is no longer there. The farmhouse where my father's father lived during his first six years outside of Litchville, North Dakota is no longer there. The address for the house where my father's father lived as a teenager once he moved into Valley City, North Dakota can't be located on any map. It's as if the building never existed. The farmhouse where my father's mother grew up in Ransom County, North Dakota is one of the few houses still standing. But when my father examines the building with me on Google Maps satellite view, he scrunches up his face, confused. He points hesitantly at the image on my laptop and explains that only the central section of the main house remains, that all the other buildings are new, that even the arrangement of the trees is different.

The childhood home where my mother spent her first nine years in Michigan City, North Dakota is no longer there. The house where she lived in high school in Grand Forks, North Dakota is no longer there. It was wiped away in a torrential flood in 1997, the worst flood in more than a hundred and fifty years — a flood of Biblical proportions, people said — when the Red River surged over its banks and engulfed the city, forcing almost every resident to flee. The house where my mother and father lived after they got married and before I was born is no longer there. The Red River Flood destroyed that one, too. The streets where those houses once stood are no longer there. Now a public park lines the river's banks, a wide-open, flat expanse of grass dotted here and there with a few trees. My mother went back a few years ago for the first time in decades and told me how she'd stood there in that park, scanning the open space, trying to make sense of it, gazing uneasily into the open air, unable to locate the exact place where her former homes once had stood, where she and my father in their naïve newlywed years, decades before they divorced, used to hold each other while they slept in the far reaches of the night, where my sister had learned to stand, then walk, where my mother's entire life had flourished, where her memories should have been resonating. But she stood, decades later, turning her head from here to there, trying to make meaning out of an absence, trying to find solace in a void.

Every one of those buildings, every one of those homes probably stood for less than fifty years. Every last one of those houses — where families lived and raised children, where they struggled, year after year, to make a living and feed their families, dragging a plow through the ground, planting corn and wheat, where people were born in their parents' bedroom and people were married in their parents' living room and where those parents died in those same bedrooms — were all left to decay and disappear over the decades, or torn down by tractor in just a few short hours, or ripped apart instantly by the torrential, God-like vengeance of a river, the cradle of an entire generation of a family reduced to rubble, decades of a collective yearning vanished into the air, the physical anchors of memory — which are the roots of the self — wiped forever off the face of the earth.

There is no architecture left to commemorate my ancestors' lives; no archeologist will ever be able to document their existence; no painter will ever bring them to life on canvas; no movie will ever do their stories justice. You cannot locate these homes on any map anymore. The closest you can get is to gaze out at photographs of vast stretches of shorn fields on the Internet, at the flat expanses of treeless Dakota farmlands, miles upon miles of mown fields, and an infinite stretch of mutating clouds, and imagine the homes that might have once stood there. You cannot go to these places. You cannot drive up to them, step out of the car, and admire them from a distance with a hushed sense of awe. You cannot walk up to them and rest your hand on their wooden surface, feel the breath of the past emanating from within. It's not that they're crumbling, or lying in ruins, or even lying dead in the ground with nothing but a tombstone. No. They're simply not there. They've disappeared so utterly that you marvel that they could have ever stood there at all. There's nothing there anymore but the emptiness that has always suffused that land. And the sky. And the clouds.

It's when I think about these houses that I remind myself about clouds, how they billow and surge, soar and drift, how their essential character is self-transformation and its conjoined twin, self-annihilation. The sky, I've begun to suspect, is the earth's mirror, and the clouds, then, are our own reflections; the clouds inhabit the heavens as we inhabit the planet, revealing back to us — if we care to notice — how we shape and transform ourselves, how we roam across the land, how we flourish and entrench ourselves, splinter and disperse, how by reimagining our singular identities we reimagine a collective, dissolving ourselves into the larger forces that billow and surge, then evaporate once more into the nothingness that gave us birth.

Architecture is our attempt to make permanent the idea of home. But buildings, too, are like the clouds. Homes, too, surge and drift; they dissipate and disappear; they break up and reform; and when they take on new shapes, we ascribe new meanings to them. In its ethereality and ephemerality, in its own longing for its inevitable extinction, the idea of home, like the idea of a cloud, has never actually existed at all.

The land is just a host, the staging ground for metamorphosis, birth and demolition; the only home the land can ever make is the home of impermanence. Over the last five hundred years, several civilizations have moved into the Great Plains and called it home: first the Mandan, Hidatsa, and Arikara, then the Lakota, and then finally and most catastrophically the Americans in the late nineteenth century. The Great Plains was the home to bison, tens of millions of them; it was where enormous herds roamed for thousands of years before human beings came and annihilated them. And the sky over the Great Plains was a territory, too, home of the passenger pigeon that used to soar in flocks so vast they covered the entire sky like a pulsating stain hundreds of miles long, three to five billion of them in North America completely annihilated by European invaders over the course of just a couple hundred years.[2]

But the almost total extinction of the bison and the total eradication of the passenger pigeon were, in fact, not that unusual. 15,000 years ago, back when glaciers a hundred feet thick covered the continent, before they began their interminable retreat to mark the end of the Pleistocene age, human beings entered the Western Hemisphere for the first time and discovered — like my ancestors fifteen thousand years later — what they thought of, erroneously, as an empty canvas ripe for their reinvention, inhabited by animals the size of giants: mastodons and wooly mammoths, a bird known as the teratorn with a wingspan wider

---

2   Robert V. Hine and John Mack Faragher, *The American West: A New Interpretive History* (New Haven: Yale University Press, 2000), 317–18, and Joel Greenberg, *A Feathered River Across the Sky: The Passenger Pigeon's Flight to Extinction* (New York: Bloomsbury, 2014), 1–7.

than the California condor, beavers taller than humans, giant pig-like tapirs, sloths like the megalonyx that could reach six feet high when they reared on their back feet, an ancient arma-dillo known as the glyptodont that was ten times bigger than any surviving armadillo, short-faced bears larger than griz-zlies, humpless camels known as the camelops bigger than any camel we know today, something called a shrub ox that weighed more than a thousand pounds and had crazy woolen hair and humongous horns, giant horses, great herds of them roaming across the Plains, the American lion and the American cheetah, giant saber-toothed cats called the smilodon that were bigger than anything anyone has ever seen in the Serengeti and which chased and fed off herds of antelope and bison — every last one of them killed off by climate change and by the onrushing hoard of human beings that entered the Western Hemisphere on land across the Bering Straits or in canoes across the northern Pacific with their sticks and spears and Clovis points, killing wher-ever they went, abetting the extermination of every species of megafauna across the continent in just a couple thousand years, human beings who spread death and destruction wherever they go, human beings whose essence is annihilation, human beings, it so often feels, who are nothing but a pestilence on the face of the Earth.[3]

And my own people were no different — nor am I. My ances-tors who'd been nothing but insignificant, poor farmers for mil-lennia were a blight and a curse as well. My own grandparents and great-grandparents and great-great-grandparents, strug-gling to survive through bitterly cold winters in sod houses or little wooden homes on 160-acre-tracts of land, deeply religious, going to church every Sunday, listening to sermons, taking com-munion, praying on their knees every night before they went to bed, reading the New Testament — he who is without sin let him cast the first stone, judge not lest ye be judged, for God so loved the world he gave his only begotten son, forgive them father

3   Anthony J. Stuart, *Vanished Giants: The Lost World of the Ice Age* (Chicago: University of Chicago Press, 2021), 67–112.

for they know not what they do — perhaps reading the Gospels together aloud sitting around the fireplace while the howling wind blew vortexes and slurries of snow outside their door, taciturn and prudent and unemotional, living the word of God, tolerant and pious and loving, even them, even these insignificant, poor, God-fearing farmers built homes only so that they could destroy them, tearing down every structure where once they had lived, raising children only so that the younger generation could turn away from them and move on, turning their backs on them so that they could build newer homes that they would later tear down, raising children who'd turn away from them and move on, turning their backs on them, generation after generation, accomplishing nothing with their lives except reimagining themselves as their parents had done and their parents had done before them, continuing the millennia-old project of continually constructing a more perfect future by dragging affliction in their wake wherever they turned.

§

I first became interested in genealogy a few years back when I was spending the summer in Berlin. I knew even then that our past couldn't answer any questions about who we are, but I couldn't help myself: I'd arrived at a point in my life where I needed to imagine myself anew. I'd just turned forty, had recently separated from a partner of almost twenty years, had started a new career, and was beginning a new book — a history of imaginary films — and I wanted to get away from life in New York so that I could reinvent myself in a place where I had no connections and no history.

Berlin seemed the ideal location. The city was, after all, an emblem for reimagination and renewal. I'd write in the morning and spend afternoons wandering on foot, imagining myself as a Benjaminian flâneur, trying to picture the city as it might have looked throughout its many earlier incarnations. But if you walked through the city when I was there, just a couple of decades after the fall of the Berlin Wall, passing gaggles of friends brunching at restaurant tables out on sidewalks, playgrounds with children scrambling over patchwork pirate ships of logs and slides and metal chains, grandmothers riding bicycles from the grocery store, and families with toddlers hanging out in beer gardens in the middle of the afternoon, you'd have no idea that the Nazis or the Communists had ever existed, much less ruled here.

Like a lot of people in my generation just entering middle age, I'd become fascinated for the first time with discovering my roots. And while I was in Berlin it occurred to me that I had, just that summer, come upon an unexpected opportunity to discover something about my origins because I had found myself, for the first time in my life, close to the place where I was born. I had not been born in Arizona or in North Dakota as many of my friends might have assumed. I was born instead — in a twist of fate brought on by the global reach of twentieth-century politics — in West Germany, because my father had been drafted at the height of the Vietnam War, had declared himself a conscientious objector, and had ended up, randomly, as a clerk at an American army base in Nuremberg. And I just happened to be born — again, arbitrarily — during the twelve-month period when he and my mother had been stationed there. And though I knew better, I couldn't avoid the innate human yearning to try to understand myself by coming face to face with the random facts that had set me on this earth.

So I planned out a journey for myself: I made a hotel reservation online, bought some train tickets, and one morning soon thereafter I was on a train heading south toward Bavaria. By that afternoon, I was standing in front of the imperial castle of Nuremberg, one of the great economic hubs of the Northern Renaissance, a place that, having grown up in a suburb on the edge of the Sonoran Desert, felt wholly fantastical to me.

The next morning, I asked the hotel to call me a taxi. In my halting German, I told the driver that I had come to the city because I had been born there decades before, and he nodded sagely, understanding instinctively the logic of my illogical quest. I told him, then, that I wanted to make two stops: first, to the apartment on the outskirts of town where I had lived with my parents and sister the first six months of my life, and second, to the site of the American army hospital outside the city center where I was born. As he walked me to the car, it became clear that his English was better than my German, but I could tell that his accent wasn't German, so I asked him where he was from, fulfilling our innate need to cultivate our shared humanity by narrating our origins to each other. And as he eased the car gently into a narrow cobblestoned street, he began the story of his own roots, throwing a glance my way now and then in the rearview mirror to make sure we were making a connection.

He had been born, he told me as we passed through the medieval center of the city, in Bosnia-Herzegovina — or, rather, he had been born in Yugoslavia, he said, correcting himself with a hint of pride, still holding on to the multiethnic ideal in which he'd been raised. It was only after he came to Germany as a refugee, he told me, that he'd started to refer to himself as a Bosnian. The Serbs started bombing Sarajevo in '92, he continued. Four people died every day. If four people had died one day, nobody would've noticed, and if four people had died every day for a week, people would've been anxious and afraid, but when four people die every day every week for four years, he said, and then he trailed off. Then, he said, then there's no words for it. Three hundred shells landed a day, thousands of buildings were turned into rubble, a third of the residents managed, somehow over the years, to sneak out, to evade the soldiers in the hills, and escape. He got out in 1995, he told me as we drove past the medieval walls of the city center out into the nineteenth-century apartment blocks on the city's periphery. He didn't want to leave home but he couldn't stay. He didn't know where he was going, he was just moving, on the run. From train station to shelter to bus station to refugee center. Huddling for a while in tents. It was the bureaucracy that transported him, made decisions for him. It was Europe, he said, that decided where he would live, what language he would need to learn, what country his children would grow up calling home. He ended up in Nuremberg purely by chance, a product of decisions made beyond his control. But he felt lucky. He'd been driving a cab here ever since. His wife had managed to join him. His sons were born here, knew nothing of the war, of Sarajevo, of Yugoslavia. And they would never know, he said, because he would never go back. He would never take them; he could never take them because Sarajevo was not Sarajevo anymore. It didn't look the same. So many of the buildings were gone, the streets had changed, his friends had all fled, his parents were dead. There was a city there, he admitted, and it did have the same name, but in truth, he said, Sarajevo was no longer there.

By then we were driving through the twentieth-century outskirts dotted with small homes that reminded me, surprisingly, of the American suburb where I'd grown up. And then, sooner than I'd expected, he turned the car into a small development, a quiet residential street, and came to a crawl along a stretch of nondescript, two-story, beige townhouses. I searched the addresses on the front doors, and counted off the numbers of each apartment out loud as we continued to roll down the street. And then we were there, stopped in front of the compact building that had once been my home. I stepped out, stood on the sidewalk, and studied the building. And the sensation was, of course, underwhelming.

At the center of this medieval city, once the wealthiest urban center of the Holy Roman Empire, the great castle still commanded the skyline, and the timbered house of Albrecht Dürer, the greatest Renaissance painter of the German lands, still stood. But in this quiet neighborhood on the outskirts of town where I had lived as a baby just forty years earlier, everything had changed. My parents told me that there used to be a bakery on the first floor, I told my driver, pacing on the sidewalk, pointing at a blank wall. My mother said that the aroma of baking bread wafted up through the house every morning. My sister used to play with the girl who lived downstairs. But the bakery was no longer there. It was hard to imagine how a bakery could even have existed there. I was trying to connect the building before me with the memory of the photographs I'd seen in the old family photo albums, but the space didn't strike any chords within me. The street was nondescript, lined with equally unremarkable homes up and down the block. The baker's family and their daughter must have moved away decades ago. Nobody was out on the sidewalk. There were no stores or playgrounds or churches where people could gather. There were no children playing out on the street.

So we turned back to the car to drive to our final destination, the site of the American army hospital, the place of my birth, and as we drove back the way we'd come, I was struck suddenly by a sense of déjà vu, struck by the nostalgic memory of riding the subway late at night after a movie, going home but not really going anywhere, since the next day would be just like the day that was coming to an end, immobilized in a circular journey, in some interstitial zone. I was on a quest, yes — but as always, a quest for an illusion. My mother had told me, before I left Berlin, that they'd torn down the American army hospital in Nuremberg years ago. The place where I was born, the symbolic site that I was searching for, she said, was no longer there. Like my mother and her mother before her, the place where I had come into the world did not exist anymore. Like my mother and her mother before her — and like everyone else on the face of the earth — I had no true birthplace, and thus no true origins.

When I asked my driver, he confirmed that it was true: the army hospital was no longer there. But he remembered the building, he said: a grand, imposing structure. He knew where it used to be, he said, and he'd point out the location to me as we drove by. Back in Berlin, I'd studied photographs of the hospital I'd managed to find on the Internet: a stolid, neo-classical structure with a six-story main building flanked by two four-story wings, a dull, unadorned emblem of Central European officiousness. So as I scanned the horizon along the road, I kept searching for an absence as grand and imposing as the building that once had stood there, an absence magnificent enough to have nurtured the identity I'd been cultivating for myself all these years. So I was surprised when, sooner than I'd expected as we sped along the two-lane highway through the suburbs on our way back to the city center, my driver lifted his left arm from the steering wheel and pointed off into the distance.

There, he said.

And I leaned forward, squinting, confused. It seemed like just another typical development of suburban houses to me, all tucked away from the traffic behind a plain brick wall. But he was pointing, I soon realized, a little higher than I'd first assumed, above the buildings, at nothing in particular, at the cloudless sky.

There, he said again. *That's where it used to be.*

And as I gazed deeper into that absence that seemed suddenly to be pulsating, I remembered what I'd read about the American army hospital online, back in Berlin. Because that building, like every work of architecture, had an origin story, too. It was not built by the Americans, but by the Wehrmacht back in 1936, just three years after Hitler had come to power, when the Nazis set out on their re-armament efforts in violation of the Versailles Treaty. And the Nazi's armed forces had decided to build their newest, finest hospital in Nuremberg, the same city where the Nazi Party held its annual rallies, where in 1935 the Party enacted the set of laws that denied citizenship to Jews, where in 1936 Leni Riefenstahl filmed the Nazi propaganda film *Triumph of the Will,* and where after the war, the Allied powers conducted the military tribunals against the Nazi leadership. But after the war, the winners were quick to shunt this origin story aside. It's so convenient and so easy, after all, to ignore the past in order to invent more comfortable conceptions of the present. After the major powers divided Germany up and set the Cold War in motion, the Americans took over the building and turned it into a hospital for their armed forces stationed across the continent, deploying the grandeur of its architecture to fashion a new narrative propelled by a new conflict of ideas. And there the building stood for another forty years, a working hospital but also an active emblem of the Cold War between the forces of democracy and communism. But then, after the fall of the Berlin Wall and the collapse of the Soviet Union brought a sudden shift in international affairs, the Americans decided they didn't need the hospital anymore. The narrative we'd made out of architecture had changed once again. In 1994 they tore it down. The American army hospital, a tool for both the Nazi government and the United States, a victim of capitalism's victory over totalitarian socialism, stood on that ground for a mere fifty-eight years. That was where my mother, who'd been raised in a town of a mere five hundred people, with a cow and chickens in her backyard, surrounded by farms out in the middle of the flattest and emptiest part of the Great Plains, the daughter of a generation raised on farms in the Dakotas, who were themselves the children of poor immigrants from Europe who'd settled in land made empty by pandemics and wars and forced relocation of its previous inhabitants, arbitrarily found herself giving birth to me. And as we passed the space where that building once stood, I stared intently into the deepest reaches of the distance where the driver was pointing, as if I could detect in the atmosphere the essence of my identity, though I knew by then that searching for one's origins in any location was a fool's errand, as if any of us could find ourselves in our origins, in our studious dedication to an image, in our woozy submission to the hypnotic unfolding of a film, or in fact, find ourselves anywhere at all, as foolish as trying to peer into a bank of clouds to discern our destination, and I kept on staring into that infinitely cloudless and colorless air, into the empty desolation that is the heavens, into the mirror of my mind's eye, and I said to myself, "Yes, I was born there. I was born in the sky."

Bibliography

Burke, Cristina E. "Waniyetu Wówapi: An Introduction to the Lakota Winter Count Tradition." In *The Years the Stars Fell: Lakota Winter Counts at the Smithsonian,* edited by Candace S. Greene and Russell Thornton, 1–11. Washington, DC: The Smithsonian Institution, 2007.

Cassavetes, John, dir. *A Woman Under the Influence.* 1974; Criterion Collection, 2013. Blu-Ray disc.

Celan, Paul. *Poems of Paul Celan: Revised and Expanded.* Translated by Michael Hamburger. New York: Persea Books, 2002.

Crane, Hart. *The Complete Poems of Hart Crane.* Edited by Marc Simon. New York: Liveright, 2000.

DeJong, David H. *Diverting the Gila: The Pima Indians and the Florence-Casa Grande Project, 1916–1928.* Tucson: University of Arizona Press, 2021.

Dreyer, Carl Theodor, dir. *Ordet.* Palladium Film, 1955; Criterion Collection, 2015. Blu-Ray Disc.

Fenn, Elizabeth A. *Encounters at the Heart of the World: A History of the Mandan People.* New York: Hill and Wang, 2014.

Fish, Suzanne K., and Paul R. Fish, eds. *The Hohokam Millennium.* Santa Fe: School for Advanced Research Press, 2007.

Greenberg, Joel. *A Feathered River Across the Sky: The Passenger Pigeon's Flight to Extinction.* New York: Bloomsbury, 2014.

Hämäläinen, Pekka. *Lakota America: A New History of Indigenous Power.* New Haven: Yale University Press, 2019.

Hawks, Howard, dir. *Only Angels Have Wings.* Columbia Pictures, 1939; Criterion Collection, 2016. Blu-Ray disc.

Hine, Robert V., and John Mack Faragher. *The American West: A New Interpretive History.* New Haven: Yale University Press, 2000.

Historical Statistics of the United States, Colonial Times to 1970, Part 1. Washington, DC: United States Bureau of the Census, 1975. https://www.census.gov/library/publications/1975/compendia/hist_stats_colonial-1970.html.

Jung, Carl. "On the Relation of Analytical Psychology to Poetry." In *The Portable Jung,* edited by Joseph Campbell, translated by R.F.C. Hull, 301–22. New York: Penguin Books, 1971.

Mann, Charles C. *1491: New Revelations of the Americas Before Columbus.* New York: Alfred A. Knopf, 2005.

Ray, Nicholas, dir. *On Dangerous Ground.* 1951; Warner Archive Collection, 2016. Blu-Ray disc.

Sontag, Susan. "In Plato's Cave." In *On Photography,* 3–24. New York: Farrar, Straus and Giroux, 1973.

Stuart, Anthony J. *Vanished Giants: The Lost World of the Ice Age.* Chicago: University of Chicago Press, 2021.

Treuer, Anton. *Ojibwe in Minnesota.* St. Paul: Minnesota Historical Society Press, 2010.

Treuer, David. *The Heartbeat of Wounded Knee: Native America from 1890 to the Present.* New York: Riverhead Books, 2019.

Vallejo, César. "Trilce XLV." Translated by Charles Tomlinson and Henry Gifford. *Poetry* 109, no. 4 (1967): 232–33. https://www.jstor.org/stable/20597974.

zu Wied, Maximilian. *People of the First Man: Life Among the Plains Indians in Their Final Days of Glory: The Firsthand Account of Prince Maximilian's Expedition Up the Missouri River, 1833–34.* Edited by Davis Thomas and Karin Ronnefeldt. Watercolors by Karl Bodmer. New York: E.P. Dutton, 1976.